BARCELONA

— in your pocket —

MAIN CONTRIBUTOR: PAUL MURPHY

PHOTOGRAPH CREDITS
Photos supplied by The Travel Library:
Stuart Black 5, 8, 9, 19, 21, 23, 25, 28, 31, 32, 35, 36, 38, 39, 41, 43, 45, 47, 53, 54, 58, 61, 65, 68, 70, 75, 84, 85, 91, 95, 98, 105, 115, 117; Alan Copson 123, 126; Vaughn Emmerson 51; Philip Enticknap 83; Ron Keet front cover, 62; Grant Pritchard back cover, title page, 7, 17, 30, 33(t, b), 37, 44, 46, 48, 49, 50, 52, 55, 56, 57(t), 57(b), 59, 60, 63, 64, 66, 67, 71, 74, 76, 79, 101, 103, 107; Clare Roberts 29, 34. Photos pages 57(b) and 62 ©ADAGP, Paris and DACS, London 1998
Other photos:
Prado, Madrid/Giraudon/Bridgeman Art Library, London 12; Musee Bargoin, Clermont Ferrand/ Lauros-Giraudon/Bridgeman Art Library, London 11; Paul Murphy 26, 72-73, 78, 81, 82, 89, 96, 108, 111, 118; Museu d'Història de la Ciutat 27.

Front cover: the spires of La Sagrada Família; back cover: Casa Batlló; title page: decorated roof of Palau Güell.

MANUFACTURE FRANÇAISE DES PNEUMATIQUES MICHELIN

Place des Carmes-Déchaux – 63000 Clermont-Ferrand (France)

© Michelin et Cie. Propriétaires-Éditeurs 1998

Dépôt légal Avril 98 – ISBN 2-06-652001-2 – ISSN 1272-1689

No part of this publication may be reproduced in any form

without the prior permission of the publisher.

Printed in Spain 3-98

MICHELIN TYRE PLC
Tourism Department
The Edward Hyde Building
38 Clarendon Road
WATFORD Herts WD1 1SX - UK
☎ (01923) 415000

MICHELIN TRAVEL PUBLICATIONS
Editorial Department
One Parkway South
GREENVILLE, SC 29615
☎ 1-800 423-0485

CONTENTS

INTRODUCTION

If you could design your own perfect European holiday city, what would your ingredients be? Historic cobbled streets oozing a medieval atmosphere; a Mediterranean climate and a Latin *joie de vivre*; beautiful beaches right on the city doorstep; a vibrant nightlife; characterful bars and eating places serving excellent food and drink that have remained true to local tradition; international-class museums and galleries; individual shops; the very best in street entertainment; a centre that you can cover mostly on foot but where the transport system is cheap and easy. Too good to be true? Take all of these facets, add breathtaking hilltop views, some of the most imaginative architectural design that the world has produced in the last hundred years, throw in for good measure an infectious dose of football fever – and there you have Barcelona.

To an extent, much of Barcelona *has* been purpose designed – initially for the International Exhibitions of 1888 and 1929 and, most crucially, for the Olympic Games of 1992. However, the important difference between Barcelona and many cities which have striven in vain to re-invent themselves is that Barcelona has successfully retained the best of its old parts and has been very good at redesigning new parts. The city is not only rare in having style and a strong direction, it also works extremely hard to make its dreams a reality. How many people (outside Catalonia) really thought the 25th Olympiad would work at all, let alone be one of the most successful ever? And who, in 1980, would have dreamed that by the mid-1990s Barcelona would have developed into one of the most stylish of Europe's capitals and even a popular beach resort?

The work is by no means finished, however, and perhaps the only major threat to the city is that it will outpace itself, that it will become too modern, too European, or (heaven forbid) too international. Right now, though, there has probably never been a better time to visit Barcelona.

The soaring spires of Barcelona's most famous landmark, La Sagrada Família.

GEOGRAPHY

Barcelona is located roughly three-quarters of the way up Spain's eastern coastline. To the south is the coastal city of Tarragona and the wetlands of the Ebro Delta; to the north is the holiday playground of the Costa Brava and France. In *costa* terms, Barcelona is halfway between the Costa Dorada (Daurada) and the lesser-known Costa del Maresme.

Catalonia, known locally as Catalunya, of which Barcelona is the capital, occupies this north-eastern corner of Spain, stretching west across the Pyrenees past Andorra, and just south of the Ebro Delta. It is an autonomous, but not independent, political unit.

The cable-car ride from Montjuïc offers superb views over Barcelona, its harbours and the coastline.

The easiest way to grasp Barcelona's physical layout and to get your bearings is to take the cable-car ride from Montjuïc to Barceloneta. To the south-east lies the hill of Montjuïc (173m/567ft), to the north-east is the highest point, Tibidabo (532m/1 745ft). The rest of the city and its hinterland, as far as the eye can see, is flat. Looking back from the sea the city's main thoroughfare is the tree-lined La Rambla, which terminates at the landmark statue of Columbus. To the right of this is the old town; above and beyond is the 19C Eixample. Along the coast to the right (heading north) are the beaches and the Port Olímpic, marked by two giant high-rise blocks.

HISTORY

Before and After the Romans

This Roman bust of a woman shows the hair ornament typical of the period (Museu d'Història de la Ciutat).

According to mythology, it was Hercules who founded Barcelona and the **Carthaginians** who named it *Barcino*, in honour of their great general Hamilcar Barca, who held this part of Spain around 237 BC. His legendary son Hannibal was to lose it to the **Romans** when, some 20 years later, he provoked them to enter Catalunya to embark upon the Second Punic War. The Roman colonisation of the Iberian peninsula took another two centuries and it became the most important territory after the homeland. Despite this, *Barcino* was not the regional centre of power. This honour went to *Tarracco* (modern-day Tarragona), which still retains many splendid Roman monuments. By comparison, Barcelona's Roman remains are slight; the walls, particularly by the cathedral, the subterranean discoveries below the Museu d'Història de la Ciutat and a handful of other remains are the only tangible reminders of this first real civilization.

After the Empire's disintegration, the **Visigoths** made Barcelona their first Spanish capital for a brief period. They were driven from the city by the all-conquering **Moors** in about 720, but Barcelona was reclaimed in 801 by the Christian **Franks** led by Louis, son of Charlemagne. The Moors retreated south, leaving even less of a legacy in the city than had the Romans, but the aftermath of the Frankish victory was to lead to the creation of a new, powerful Barcelona.

City of the Counts

To protect themselves against Moorish raids,

the Franks created a buffer zone covering the north of modern-day Catalunya, which they named *Marca Hispánica* (the Spanish March, or frontier). This was divided up and given to a number of their **counts** who were charged with its defence. In 878 Count Guifré el Pelós (Wilfred the Hairy) succeeded in uniting the area, made Barcelona his capital and thus founded the *Ciutat de Condes* (**City of the Counts**), a title still used today. As the Frankish empire declined, so the *Marca Hispánica* became more isolated and in 988 the Counts of Barcelona declared independence for the region.

By the year 1000 Barcelona was a city of around 6 000 people and, although still operating a feudal system, in 1070 it produced the *Usatges*, the first legal code in Europe to grant commoners equal rights with nobles (pre-dating Magna Charta by 145 years). Catalunya was also expanding: by commercial treaties; by force of arms – driving the Moors further south; and by the marriage of Ramon Berenguer IV to Petronilla, Queen of Aragon, thus uniting Catalunya and Aragon to form the **Crown of Aragon**, ruled by the Catalan Count-Kings. Their son, **Alfons II**, chose Barcelona as the capital city and was the first Count of Barcelona and King of Aragon. Most successful of the Count-Kings was **Jaume I** (1213-1276), who became known as "The Conqueror'. Between 1229 and 1235 he cleared the Moors from the Balearic Islands and in 1238 extended the Catalunya-Aragon empire south to Valencia.

In 1282 Jaume's son, **Pere II** of Barcelona ('the Great'), added Sicily to the empire by political manoeuvring, and this became a

Jaume I, the Conqueror, was responsible for the greatest expansion of the Catalan Empire, with Barcelona as its centre.

9

new base for commercial and military expansionism. The Catalan mercenary forces (*Almogàvers*) became feared throughout the Mediterranean, and by 1324 Corsica and Sardinia were also under the red-and-yellow striped banner of Catalunya. This was Barcelona's Golden Age, with the city's growing status and wealth reflected in the bold Catalan-Gothic architecture of Santa Maria del Mar and the cathedral, the enormous Drassanes shipyards, and other beautiful buildings such as the Saló del Tinell.

Decline and Fall

All was far from well, however: civil and social unrest was a daily fact of life, the upkeep of the Mediterranean colonies was proving very costly (particularly the belligerent island of Sardinia), and in the 1340s the Black Death devastated the region.

In 1410 Martin I ('the Humane') died heirless and so brought to an end the 500-year unbroken line of the Counts of Barcelona. A Castilian prince ascended the throne and by the time of the reign of his grandson, Joan II, Castilian influences had inexorably infiltrated the corridors of Catalan power and Mediterranean dominance had been ceded to Genoa and Venice.

Joan's son was **Prince Ferdinand** who, in 1469, married **Isabella of Castile**. The joining of Catalunya-Aragon to Castile was a fateful move for Catalunya. While its powers were waning, its larger, richer partner was in the ascendancy. Even the triumphal reception of **Columbus** by Ferdinand and Isabella in Barcelona in 1493 was to prove disastrous to the city. The Mediterranean

The reception of Columbus by Ferdinand and Isabella, 1493.

henceforth lost much of its importance and only the southern Spanish ports were allowed to reap the New World dividends. The following year the dreaded Inquisition

further impoverished the city by expelling its Jews, and administrative powers formally passed to Castile.

While Castile was enjoying Spain's Golden Age, quite literally, thanks to the *conquistador* treasures flowing in from the New World, Catalunya and Barcelona continued to decline. Gradually, the country's wealth was squandered on a series of **wars** with France, England and other European powers, and

Philip V, who defeated Barcelona in 1714 after a 13-month siege, created 'Spain' as a unitary state.

the need to tax Catalunya became paramount. When Spain and France went to war again in 1635, Catalunya rebelled against Castilian taxes and declared itself under the protection of the French, in what became known as the **War of the Reapers**. But Catalunya had backed the losing side and in 1652 Barcelona surrendered to the Spanish forces.

Less than 50 years later Catalunya was again embroiled in civil war, this time provoked by the crisis of succession of the heirless Habsburg king, **Carlos II**. Again it chose the wrong side. In 1714, after a year of siege it capitulated to the Bourbon King, **Philip V**, who commissioned a formidable fortress, La Ciutadella, to intimidate and watch over the people. The Catalan language was proscribed, the universities closed and the governing institutions of the Generalitat and its councils were abolished.

Recovery and Expansion

For much of the 18C Catalunya effectively disappeared as a political entity, subsumed within the larger Spain, though its economy and the port of Barcelona in particular steadily improved. In 1778 it was allowed (for the first time) to trade with the Americas, and industrialisation, based on the import of American cotton, began. The **Peninsular War** (or Liberation War) of 1808-1814 once again gave Catalunya the chance to side with an anti-Spanish army. Napoleon promised to restore autonomy to the region if it would support him. For once Catalunya pledged its allegiance wisely and although Montserrat was sacked, Barcelona escaped great damage and, with the help of the

British, Napoleon was defeated.

During the early and mid-19C Catalunya was in the vanguard of Spain's **industrial revolution**. In 1832 Barcelona saw the country's first steam-driven mill and in 1848 the country's first railway. Olive oil, wine and textiles became major industries supplying Spain and overseas. There was also a resurgence in the **Catalan culture** and the language was revived. For the working classes however, life was hard and often brutish; during the mid-19C Barcelona was a hotbed of social unrest and the scene of many bloody repressions.

A landmark event in the city's physical development occurred in 1854 when it was finally allowed to break free from its 14C city wall confines. The new town, planned in a grid fashion to the north, was known simply as the **Eixample** (the Expansion) and towards the end of the century many of its buildings were handsomely embellished and designed by the *modernisme* movement. This was an era of growth, self-confidence and prosperity, which saw the transformation of the city to its modern-day appearance. To celebrate, Barcelona staged the **Universal Exhibition** of 1888, demolishing the hated Ciutadella and creating in its place a beautiful city park.

Wars and Repression

Meanwhile, the country as a whole lurched from crisis (the First Carlist War of 1833-1839) to crisis (the Second Carlist War of 1875) to crisis (the Spanish-American War of 1898). Catalan discontent at national affairs came to a head in 1909 over the conscription of troops to fight in Morocco, and during the ensuing riots in what came to be known as *Setmana Tràgica* (Tragic Week) over 100 people died. Ironically, Europe's greatest upheaval, the **First World War**, proved a boost to the Catalan economy, which supplied the French war effort, and Barcelona became a haven for intellectual refugees, enhancing its growing fashionable cultural reputation. Yet social unrest increased, with violent union-employee confrontations resulting in an estimated 800 casualties between 1918 and 1923. In a bid to stabilise the ever-worsening domestic and international situation – Spain was now embroiled in Morocco – in 1923 **Primo de Rivera**, the Captain-General of Catalunya and Barcelona, staged a **coup** and established a military dictatorship, though the monarchy was retained.

In 1929 Barcelona again became an international showcase, successfully hosting the **International Exhibition** which sparked off a great bout of civil engineering projects, including the metro underground railway. The following year Primo de Rivera resigned, the monarchy abdicated and Catalunya declared independence from Madrid. Unfortunately the political situation was becoming more volatile than ever and in 1936, with the country sliding towards anarchy, **General Franco** staged the military coup which was to result in the **Spanish Civil War**. Barcelona's military was initially supportive of Franco but they were suppressed by a popular civil guard movement and the city continued as a Republican stronghold until 1939 when it was bombed, with the loss of some 2 000 buildings, and fell to the Nationalists.

Post-Civil War Spain, with over half a million dead, was in tatters. The Catalan culture was once again suppressed and the economy languished. Despite this, a strong groundswell of Catalan nationalism remained and manifested itself in various peaceful anti-government protests and gestures.

Rebirth and World Fame

Following Franco's death in 1975 and the restoration of the monarchy, **democracy** slowly returned to Spain. In 1978 Barcelona saw the re-establishment of its Generalitat as the head of the autonomous (but not independent) Catalunya.

Spain entered the European Community in 1986 and began to astonish its affluent north European neighbours with its phenomenal **economic growth** rate, led in no small part by Barcelona. Eyebrows were raised further that year when the city was awarded the **1992 Olympic Games**, and serious doubts were expressed at home and abroad during the six-year preparation period. By the end of the 25th Olympiad, however, there was near-unanimous agreement that this had been one of the most visually stunning, best-organised games ever. Barcelona, beamed nightly to millions of living rooms throughout the world, was now firmly established on the map and in the world's mind. As in 1929, the Games were used to kick-start many major civil engineering projects, including new ring roads, major renovation and clean-up works and, most obviously (to the visitor who knew Barcelona before 1992), the opening up of the city to the sea. The Port Olímpic leisure area and the new beaches are important tourist dividends from 1992, recently augmented by the Port Vell developments.

As Barcelona approaches the millennium, it is with a degree of optimism not seen in centuries. The Catalan culture has never been stronger, the city infrastructure has never been in better shape and the economy is now buoyed up by record visitor numbers. Once again it can count itself among the world's great cities.

PEOPLE AND CULTURE

The stereotypical Spanish view of a Barcelonan is someone who works too hard, has little sense of fun and is cold to outsiders. Yet ask any foreign holiday visitor their opinion and they will almost certainly say the opposite. As the 1992 Olympics demonstrated, Catalans have always been hard workers, but they play hard too. Witness the city's famous designer bars,

Old friends enjoy a quiet moment in the park.

packed until the early hours, attend any of the city's 100-plus annual festivals, or just look around at the enormous sense of fun and vitality to be found on practically every square off La Rambla and the old town areas.

As for being cold, the reception visitors get – in shops, bars, restaurants or wherever – is usually both polite and friendly. It's good for business after all, and the Catalans have always been very good at business, achieving by stealth what is not possible by force.

The city has a long tradition of attracting artists and intellectuals. During the First World War it was a refuge and in the Spanish Civil War it was a rallying point for anti-Fascist romantics of all persuasions. Gaudí and his contemporaries created some of the most astonishing decorative art in the western world, Picasso spent his formative years here, while Miró has recently entered the public consciousness by the back door, with his works adapted into commercial symbols. Latterly, we have the phenomenon of designer bars, though these are just one aspect of the city's love affair with the designer in the last two decades. Right from your very first impressions, of tourist board brochures, or of Barcelona Airport, you cannot fail to be struck by the style-consciousness of the city and all that is connected with it. Indeed, in the 1990s Barcelona has almost become a byword for style, uttered in the same breath as 'made in Italy'.

Nevertheless, for all their individual showmanship, Catalans exhibit a sense of solidarity and local pride rarely found in the new Europe, where regions and nations seem to be blending ever closer. Barcelona

Football Club isn't just 11 men kicking a ball (though never even whisper as much in the Camp Nou!), nor is the *sardana* a mere dance. These are symbols of an extended family, of loyalty and friendship and collective strength.

The Sardana

The Catalan *sardana* was born in its current form around 1850, thanks largely to the efforts of the Figueras musician, Pep

The famous sardana is performed outside the Cathedral, where it never fails to attract a large crowd of on-lookers, fascinated by this Catalan tradition.

Ventura (who is honoured by the name of a Barcelona metro station). It was he who devised the steps and assembled the *cobla*, the traditional 12-piece *sardana* band, generally comprised of crusty aged gentlemen who look so old that they may have known Pep Ventura personally. Its origins in fact go back centuries, perhaps to ancient Greece, and its name comes from the *ballo sardo* dance of Sardinia, an island long held by the Catalan empire.

The participants join together in a circle, hold their hands high and dance slow but very measured and very exact steps. As one commentator has wryly pointed out, it's rather like a folk dance devised by a mathematician.

Today the *sardana* is part of the Catalan way of life, danced in every village, usually on Sunday mornings in the main square (in front of the Cathedral in Barcelona). And, although not apparent to the outsider, there are many different forms of *sardana* and competitions are held. Above all, however, it remains, alongside the Catalan language and flag, one of the region's most potent symbols of solidarity and independence.

Language

Catalan is a language originated from the Provençal region of France, with literary roots going back to the 11C and the *troubadors* (lyric court poets) of Provence. Its greatest proponent was the theologist and poet, **Ramon Llull** (1235-1316), and its literature reached a peak during the late 15C, concluding with the Catalan Golden Age. With the subsequent dominance of Castile (and hence the Castilian language) Catalan became of minor importance and was only revived in the 1830s with the *renaixença* (renaissance) of Catalan culture. During Franco's regime it was proscribed as a statement of opposition and to speak it was to court death.

Today the Catalan language is said to be the fastest growing in the world, with some 6 million speakers and an ever-expanding list of media and publications. Barcelona itself is officially bilingual (Castilian and Catalan), with around 60 per cent of the city speaking Catalan. As a foreign visitor, do not be too concerned: Castilian Spanish will do fine and will have no negative connotations. A phrase or two in Catalan, however, will certainly be appreciated!

Catalan traditions are proudly upheld, through dance, music, costume and language.

Modernisme and Antoni Gaudí

Modernisme is the Catalan version of the French art nouveau movement, developed in the late 19C and in fashion until the First World War. Adopting the characteristic swelling sinuous outlines and stylized natural forms of art nouveau, the Catalan movement was also to revive traditional crafts such as metal-working, wood-working, ceramics, stone-carving and stained glass, and put these to stunning new uses, particularly in the field of decorative art.

The classic *modernista* designer is generally agreed to be **Lluís Domènech i Montaner** (1850-1923) whose **Palau de la Música Catalana** is probably the definitive building of the period. However, the most innovative and certainly best-known designer was **Antoni Gaudí** (1852-1926). **La Sagrada Família**, **Casa Milà** (La Pedrera), **Palau Güell** and **Parc Güell** are the best showcases of his boundless imagination, blending into this new movement exuberant Arabic, Moorish,

Gothic and natural influences, together with flights of pure fantasy, to produce works of stunning individuality. Gaudí's signature decoration was the use of *trencadis*, broken mosaic fragments. At the same time, he was a superb engineer and his buildings were highly functional.

Originally a metal-worker, the deeply religious Gaudí began work on his beloved Sagrada Família in 1883, but made his reputation with his works for the industrialist Eusebi Güell, before returning to his *magnus opus*. Always something of a loner, and quite eccentric, he lived as a virtual recluse during the last decade or so of his life.

To learn more about Gaudí, visit the **Espai Gaudí** at La Pedrera and the Museu de la Sagrada Família. To see more of Barcelona's *Modernisme*, pick up the *Ruta del Modernisme* leaflet (available at the Palau Güell, Casa Lleó i Morera and other places) and enquire about the multi-ticket which offers discounts at these and other *modernista* sights open to the public.

Mosaic obelisks on the roof of Palau Güell.

23

MUST SEE

A newcomer to Barcelona may need some help in choosing what to see in and around the city. Here is a selection of sights to include on any first visit.

La Sagrada Família★★★ (Church of the Holy Family)

One of the ecclesiastical architecture wonders of this century and the city's unofficial symbol. Whatever your tastes, you can't help but be impressed by Gaudí's masterpiece, which is still not completed.

Fundació Joan Miró★★★ (Miró Foundation)

Miró is 20C Barcelona's signature artist and this is his definitive collection, housed in an attractive setting and sympathetically designed building.

Barri Gotic★★ (Gothic Quarter)

Alleyways and narrow streets lined with eating and drinking places sit side-by-side with magnificent Gothic palaces, façades and buildings, such as the **Cathedral★**. Stroll through the streets, which echo with the sound of Spanish guitars, and take in old Barcelona at its most atmospheric.

Palau Güell★★

The building that made Gaudí's name reflects him at his theatrical best here. The dark 'Gothick' house is a treat to explore, both for the architecture and furniture.

Eixample★★ and Modernist Architecture

The best way to explore the area is on foot: a stroll along **Passeig de Gràcia★★**, Barcelona's most fashionable street, is like a crash-course

in *modernista* architecture. Gaudí's genius is superbly explained in the **Casa Milà★★★** and **Casa Batlló★★**. Complete the tour by dropping in at one of the many designer nightspots in this area.

Distinctive wrought-iron balconies punctuate the curving façade of Casa Milà.

Parc de la Ciutadella★
The green heart of Barcelona, the Ciutadella Park is a glorious escape from the city's bustle and traffic. Take a walk, row a boat, enjoy the statuary, visit a museum.

Palau Nacional and Museu Nacional d'Art de Catalunya★★★
The spectacular palatial building perched on the hillside of Montjuïc is a fitting home to a world-class collection of ecclesiastic art. The recovered Romanesque church frescoes are remarkable.

La Rambla★★

The best free show in town, this world-famous street is the quintessential Barcelona promenade, combining the city's inimitable verve, flair, sense of humour and energy. Just off it are plenty of sightseeing opportunities.

Barcelona's famous pedestrian way, La Rambla, is the focus of activity of all descriptions.

Museu Picasso★

Set deep in the heart of the old city in three magnificent medieval palaces this collection is hugely enjoyable, displaying around 500 of Picasso's works from various periods.

Les Drassanes★★ and Museu Marítim★

It is not too difficult to visualise the might of Barcelona's once-great maritime prowess once you have visited this colourful collection, housed in the world's finest surviving medieval shipyard building. The mighty war galley of Don Juan de Austria is a memorable sight.

CIUTAT VELLA
(THE OLD TOWN)

Barri Gòtic★★ (Gothic Quarter)
Huddled around the cathedral, the **Barri Gòtic★★** is the heart of the old town, a labyrinth of narrow atmospheric alleyways where the sun rarely penetrates. The logical place to start to get a feel for the history of the city is at the **Museu d'Història de la Ciutat★** (City History Museum), just off the historic **Plaça del Rei★★**, at one time the courtyard of the Royal Palace belonging to the counts of Barcelona; the admission ticket also includes other buildings in the Plaça del Rei that you will want to explore. A key part of any visit to the museum should include the large subterranean complex of **Roman★★** and later remains in the Carrer dels Comtes.

Other palace buildings include the **Saló del Tinell**, a superb vaulted hall once used by the Inquisition, and the **Capella de Santa Agueda★** (St Agatha's Chapel), bare but quite beautiful and very atmospheric, with a superb 15C **retable★★**. The chapel also gives

Remains of the early Christian Basilica (5C) situated at the subterranean archaeological site in the Carrer dels Comtes (Museu d'Història de la Ciutat).

Part of the Museu d'Història de la Ciutat, the Mirador del Rei Martí can be climbed for splendid roof-top views.

access to the **Mirador del Rei Martí** (King Martin's Tower), a series of ever-ascending galleries which offer fine close-up **views★★** of the adjacent cathedral roof and spires. According to tradition it was on the steps outside these buildings, leading into the Plaça del Rei, that the Catholic monarchs Ferdinand and Isabella received Columbus in 1493, on his return from his first voyage to the New World.

The other part of the old palace complex open to the public is the courtyard and stairs of the **Palau del Lloctinent**, the Lloctinent being the Castilian king's viceroy, or representative. This is a beautiful area with a fine coffered ceiling which, together with the Plaça del Rei, often echoes with the sounds of busking classical guitarists.

Opposite here the **Catedral★** (or **La Seu**) (MX) is a huge, atmospheric, time-blackened building, hemmed in on three sides with its handsome front opening onto Plaça Nova. It dates largely from 1298 to 1430, though its façade was not finally completed until 1913. The most interesting of its many monuments are the **chest tombs** of Ramon

Somewhat drab by day, floodlighting emphasises the full beauty of the Gothic façade of the Cathedral.

Berenguer I (one of the early Counts of Barcelona 1018-1025, and the founder of the cathedral) and his wife, and the **crypt★** of its patron, Santa Eulàlia. The church is very well lit and a visit to its gloriously carved **choir★★** is well worth the small donation fee. The highlight for most visitors, however, is the **cloister★**, one of the most serene spots in the Gothic Quarter. Tall palms rise between soaring arches, flowers provide splashes of colour against sun-dappled brickwork, fountains tinkle peacefully and white geese, whose time-honoured presence is linked to the legend of Santa Eulàlia, introduce an unusual pastoral note. Off here the small **Museu de la Catedral** is worth visiting to see the inside of the 17C Chapter House and its

The tall, slender pillars and high vaulted ceilings create an awe-inspiring sense of space in the Cathedral's interior.

masterpiece by Bartolomé Bermejo, *La Pietat* (the Devotion), dating from 1490.

Close by, with an entrance in Plaça Sant Iu, is another excellent collection, the **Museu Frederic Marès★** (MX). A talented sculptor and inveterate collector, Marès has amassed here a huge **collection★** of 12C-14C polychrome wooden crucifixes and calvaries and some remarkable tombs and church porticoes. Upstairs (sadly not always open) is the **Museu Sentimental** part of the collection, a hugely enjoyable rag-bag of daily items from Barcelona life spanning the 15C to 20C. The **Café Estiu** (Summer Cafe) in the medieval courtyard is also a treat (open Easter to September).

There's another charming fountain- and palm-filled cloister in the **Casa de l'Ardiaca★**, by the front of the cathedral. This lovely house was built between the 12C and 15C for the archdeacon. Walk along the **Carrer**

The delightful fountain and courtyard of the Casa de l'Ardiaca offers a quiet retreat from the Barri Gòtic's bustling narrow streets.

31

del Bisbe (Bishop's Street) and look up to see Barcelona's 'Bridge of Sighs', an intricately carved neo-Gothic gallery which crosses the street. It was fashioned in 1929 as part of the area's rejuvenation scheme for the 1929 International Exhibition. Carrer del Bisbe leads to the large, open square of **Plaça Sant Jaume**, where the important civic institutions of the **Ajuntament** (City Hall) and the **Palau de la Generalitat** (Catalan Government Headquarters) face each other.

Parts of the Ajuntament are open on weekend mornings (when there are no official events taking place) and are well worth a visit. Here you can see staircases, courtyards, the Hall of Chronicles, the Room of the Queen Regent and the glorious stone-vaulted 14C **Saló de Cent★**, where the Council of One Hundred (the city's body of 100 medieval councillors) sat. Step around the corner into Carrer de la Ciutat to see the beautiful Gothic façade of the Saló de Cent.

Spanish and Catalan flags fly side by side on the Ajuntament.

La Ribera

Cross the Vía Laietana east and you are in
La Ribera (MNVX), the original suburb of
the walled city. Its finest street is **Carrer de
Montcada★★**, a whole row of beautifully
preserved medieval palaces, some of which
are open to the public. The finest example is
the **Palau Berenguer d'Aguilar★** which
houses the **Museu Picasso★**. Although few of
Picasso's most famous works are here it is
still the most visited museum in the city.
Picasso lived in Barcelona during his
formative years (from the age of 14 to 23)
and painted the greater part of his Blue
Period works (1901-1904) while here. The
museum reflects this early time (including
some splendid un-Picasso-like realist
paintings) then fast-forwards to later Cubist
works and jumps again to the late 1950s with
his famous series, *Las Meninas*, based on
Velázquez's masterpiece.

Just across the street are two more
museums. The **Museu Tèxtil i
d'Indumentària** (Museum of Textiles and
Fashion) features a collection of fabrics and
fashions from over the centuries, worth
seeing just for the palace it occupies, and for
the **Café Tèxtil** set in its beautiful courtyard.

*Typical narrow
streets in the Old
Town.*

*The Picasso
Museum is housed
in a series of
medieval palaces,
linked by charming
courtyards.*

The purity of lines in the lovely Santa Maria del Mar have led this to be considered the finest example of Catalan-Gothic architecture.

Adjacent is the new **Museu Barbier-Mueller** ethnological museum, with a permanent **pre-Colombian** display and rotating exhibitions. Its fascinating objects are superbly displayed in darkened rooms.

Other former palaces along Carrer de Montcada house art galleries (such as the Galeria Maeght in the Casa Cervelló Giudice, and the Galeria Surrealista which has Dalí, Miró and Picasso), shops and refreshment stops, the most notable being **El Xampanyet**. Next door is the **Palau Dalmases**, with a glorious patio and **frieze-decorated stairway★**. You can enjoy a drink and listen to classical music here at its **Espai Barroc** (Baroque Space) bar in the evening.

At the bottom of Carrer de Montcada is the beautiful church of **Santa Maria del Mar★★** (NX). Built in the 14C, when this part of the city was on the seafront and

Catalunya was a great maritime power, this was the sailors' and merchants' principal church. It is held to be the most perfect example of Catalan-Gothic architecture, with a design (based on precise mathematical calculation) incorporating slender soaring pillars, a wide nave and narrow aisles which combine to produce a sense of great harmony. Large stained-glass windows illuminate the airy upper spaces.

In the northern section of La Ribera, just off Vía Laietana, is the **Palau de la Música Catalana★★** (MV) (Palace of Catalan Music), the city's principal concert hall and its most astonishing example of *modernista* architecture (*see* p.22). Built in 1908, it is the work of Lluís Domènech i Montaner; and if you think the **exterior mosaics★** are spectacular (they represent Catalan traditional music), wait until you see the interior. A mosaic-relief of the muses playing

An outstanding display of mosaics decorate the façade of the modernista Palau de la Música Catalana.

musical instruments, a forest of rainbow-glazed stone columns and a fantastic **inverted cupola**★★ in multi-coloured glass are just a few of the treats in an uninhibited riot of eye-popping colour and sculpture. (*Tours are conducted Monday to Friday at 2pm and 3pm, also at 3.30pm and 4pm in July; closed August.*)

LA RAMBLA★★

La Rambla★★ (LVMY), the most famous street in the city, is a broad, tree-lined boulevard that stretches from Plaça de Catalunya to the statue of Columbus on the waterfront. Its name has nothing to do with the thousands who ramble along here daily, but is derived from the Arabic word (*ramla*)

The tree-lined La Rambla snakes its way through the heart of the city.

for dry river bed. Cars do pass along each side of La Rambla, but they are greatly outnumbered by pedestrians who at peak times turn the broad central boulevard into a throning jammed mass of humanity. This is much more than just a street – it is a fashion walk, an al fresco café, an outdoor market, a pop-art gallery and, above all, a theatrical experience. Like all good shows it changes frequently but look out for well-established local characters such as the ancient busker with a hurdy-gurdy and a tiny dog dressed in a *Barça* football shirt, the aged and sadly pathetic flamenco dancer from Andalucía and a whole host of unblinking, rock-solid 'human statues' ranging from a silver-sprayed Don Quixote to a greasily quiffed Elvis Presley, to perhaps a trio of invisible men 'bandaged' head to toe in *El País*, while at the bottom of La Rambla a rotund entrepreneur does a very passable impression of Columbus himself. Just throw a coin to alter their poses.

A human statue on La Rambla, one of the many amusing free entertainments to be found along the promenade.

Starting at the north end of La Rambla, **Plaça de Catalunya** is a huge square with some handsome fountains and statuary, and often resounds to the sound of musicians of all nationalities. Also here is the tourist office, the ever-popular **Hard Rock Café**, the famous department store **El Corte Inglés** (which offers an excellent view from its ninth-floor terrace restaurant) and the **Café Zurich**, a time-honoured Barcelona meeting place (due to reopen in 1998).

The first section of La Rambla is the **Rambla de Canaletes** (LV 27). Legend has it that if you drink from its iron fountain you will never leave Barcelona (or at least you will certainly return). Next is the **Rambla dels Estudis** (LX), famous for its caged birds, and then the picturesque **Rambla de les Flors** with its multitude of flower-sellers.

The architecture (with several *modernista* and turn-of-the-century flourishes) at the top end of La Rambla is worth craning your neck for. One unmissable building is the large 18C **Palau de la Virreina★**, the only palace on La Rambla which is open to visitors, hosting temporary exhibitions of various kinds.

People aside, the most colourful part of La Rambla is undoubtedly the **Mercat de Sant Josep** (St Joseph's Market), better known as **La Boquería** (LX). Housed beneath a beautiful Victorian wrought-iron canopy, this is the city's principal fresh produce market and its smells, colours, banter and bustle are a feast for all the senses (*open Monday to Saturday*). There are also some good places to snack and eat in here. The Boquería is at the midway point of La Rambla, which is marked by a pavement mosaic by Joan Miró. Look out too for the landmark **Casa Bruno Quadros** (No 82),

La Boquería is a riot of colours, smells and sounds – with fresh produce to suit all tastes.

A fearsome dragon guards the Casa Bruno Quadros, alongside a large umbrella indicating a former use of the shop.

built in the 1890s and decorated with flamboyant umbrella designs (recalling its original function as an umbrella shop) and an enigmatic Chinese-style dragon.

Just below the Boquería is what was once the most elegant of all La Rambla's buildings, the **Gran Teatre del Liceu★,** destroyed by fire in 1994. Rebuilding work has taken longer than expected and this famous opera house is now scheduled to reopen for the 1998-99 season. Opposite is another famous institution, the *fin-de-siècle* **Café de l'Opera**, an atmospheric place for a rest and refreshments.

A few metres south, off the left-hand side of La Rambla, is the **Plaça Reial★★** (MY). This is one of Barcelona's finest squares, surrounded by handsome high arcaded buildings and adorned with tall palms and fancy lampstands by the young Antoni Gaudí. Once notorious as the haunt of the city's low life, the square is a fashionable place once again, full of good restaurants, bars and nightspots; do take the usual personal security precautions though.

The bottom section of La Rambla, where there are still a couple of sex shops and some dubious characters, was also once infamous as the hunting grounds of pickpockets and muggers; and immediately to the right (west) is the **Barri Chino** (LY) (Chinese Quarter), so named because of its former shanty-town atmosphere – there never was a Chinese population here. Things have been cleaned up considerably in recent years but you can still get a taste of its rather seedy ambience, if you wish, by taking an early evening stroll along Carrer Santa Mónica. Outside the **Café Pastis**, a splendid old-time French-style bar straight from Paris's Montmartre and the days of Edith Piaf, transvestite prostitutes strut for trade. Don't wander too far abroad in this area late at night.

Back on La Rambla is the **Santa Mónica Convent**, now an art centre where contemporary exhibitions are staged on a rotating basis (*open daily*). Almost opposite is the **Museu de Cera** (Wax Museum, *open daily*). The so-called likenesses of many of the world-famous figures are somewhat disappointing and a much better bet would be to pop into the adjacent **Bosque de les Fades** (Fairies' Wood) café-bar. This is one

Surrounded by tall, gracious buildings, the elegant Plaça Reial is a popular meeting place and is home to stamp and coin markets at weekends.

of the city's stranger designer bars, based on an Alice in Wonderland-cum-enchanted forest theme. Children will love it!

La Rambla finishes at the monument to Columbus (*see* p.45).

Off La Rambla★★ (north to south)
Strike off right, away from the noisy bird cages of La Rambla, along Calle Bonsuccés into the **Raval** district (CS) to find a huge luminous glass and white-walled box of a building. This is the home of the **Museu d'Art Contemporàni de Barcelona★★** or MACBA (Museum of Contemporary Art, *closed Tuesday*), one of the city's newest collections, opened in 1995. If your idea of art is pretty pictures in wooden frames be warned that MACBA will stretch you to the limit! Reviews of its exhibitions so far have been mixed but fans of the cutting-edge of late 20C contemporary art will no doubt find it stimulating. Most of the exhibits are temporary, but the permanent collection includes paintings representing styles from 1940 to the present, such as the *Dau al Set*, neo-expressionism, non-formalism and the conceptual art with works by Tàpies, Antoni Clavé, J P Viladecans and Miguel Barceló. Adjacent is the **Centre de Cultura Contemporània de Barcelona** or CCCB (Contemporary Culture Centre), intriguingly housed in the 15C **Casa de la Caritat** (House of Charity) building which boasts a charming original **patio★**. The centre shares the philosophy of MACBA and hosts rotating art exhibitions, with a cinema and concert hall (*closed Tuesday*).

Off the opposite left-hand side of La Rambla, at Plaça Bouquería, take Cardinal Casañas to **Santa Maria del Pi★** (LX). The

interior★ of this atmospheric church is another good example of Catalan-Gothic architecture, with a huge rose window over the main entrance and a fine Gothic door. The square of **Plaça del Pi** has only a solitary eponymous pine now, but it is a lively gathering point, particularly on a Thursday when there is an art market here. The adjacent square of **Plaça de Sant Josep Oriol★**, home to the famous Bar del Pi also attracts young artists and musicians.

If MACBA and the CCCB sound a little daunting, try the innovative yet far more accessible late 19C art and architecture at the **Palau Güell★★**, created by Antoni Gaudí

Local artists offer their works for sale outside the 14C Santa Maria del Pi.

Stepped brick columns and archways in the basement of Gaudí's Palau Güell.

between 1886 and 1890 (*closed Sunday*). This was the work that first made his name and here more than in any of his other creations Gaudí shows off his iron-working skills to wonderful effect. The parabolic arches in the entrance hall are a foretaste of his work to come in the Parc Güell (*see* p.75), and the weird roofscape (over which you can wander) is like a rehearsal for La Pedrera (*see* p.67). It was built as a family home for Gaudí's patron, the wealthy industrialist Eusebi Güell.

THE WATERFRONT

More than any other part of the city, the waterfront (MNY) epitomises the new post-Olympics Barcelona. The city that turned its back on its seaside and maritime heritage has, in less than a decade, become a beach resort and revitalised its old port, turning it into a major attraction for both locals and tourists.

The **Monument a Colón** (MY) (Monument to Columbus), built in 1888, is the obvious starting point for a waterside foray. No matter that Columbus was a Genoan, or even that his statue points to North Africa

Barcelona's tribute to the great explorer, Columbus, offers good views over the old shipyards and beyond.

The medieval shipyards are home to the evocative Maritime Museum, which explores Barcelona's sea-faring past.

(instead of to the New World); for some reason the Catalans claim him for their own. At least it was in Barcelona where he was received in pomp, though ironically the discovery of the New World initially impoverished the city (*see* p.12). You can ascend the 50m (164ft) iron statue by lift (*the entrance is underground, open daily*) but the views are through glass and it can be unpleasantly crowded up there. However, this is a good place to appreciate the scale of the old **Drassanes**★★ (shipyards) immediately below. Dating from the late 13C and 14C, they are the largest surviving medieval shipyards in the world and are now home to the excellent **Museu Marítim★** (Maritime Museum). The spectacular centrepiece is a reconstruction of the last great war galley, the Royal Galley of Don Juan of Austria, which was rowed into action to save Christendom at the crucial Battle of Lepanto in 1571. An entertaining audio tour brings this and other aspects of the museum to life.

A new swing bridge connects the end of La Rambla to the small promontory of the **Port Vell★** (Old Port). On summer evenings this becomes a virtual extension of La Rambla, with thousands crossing the water, alongside the marina of the prestigious Reial Club Marítim and Club Nàutic, to enjoy themselves at the newly created Port Vell entertainment zone. This centres around the **Maremagnum** complex, which features a whole host of trendy shopping and eating options. The biggest single attraction is the brand new state-of-the-art **Aquàrium**, the

All aboard a golondrina for a tour of Port Vell and the harbour.

47

Those with a head for heights can pick out the city's landmarks from the comfort of a cable-car.

largest, and probably the best, aquarium in Europe (*open daily*). There are 21 large-scale tanks exhibiting marine life from all over the world, culminating in an exciting shark tunnel. Equally dramatic is the Port Vell's **IMAX** cinema, where special films (sometimes in 3-D) are projected onto a massive screen which is curved through 180° and sucks you right into the middle of the action.

There are two ways to see more of the harbour. The traditional option is aboard a *golondrina* (swallow) **excursion boat** which makes a 30-minute port circuit (excursion boats also offer a two-hour excursion to the Port Olímpic). This is a pleasant enough trip and although there is often not a great deal to see, at least you get a feel for the size of some of the massive ships that use the commercial port of Barcelona. For a seagull's view, take the **Transbordador Aeri** (cable-car). The full circuit runs from Plaça

Armada, at the foot of Montjuïc, via the Torre Jaume I, on the Moll Barcelona, and across the port to the Torre San Sebastià, overlooking the beach of Platja San Sebastià. The views are magnificent and you can go to and from whichever tower you wish; if you don't want to ride in the cable-car, you can still ascend either of the 80m (262ft)-tall towers by elevator just for the view.

The city **beaches** are excellent, comprising wide stretches of imported golden sand – well-cared for and watched over by lifeguards – with boardwalks, showers and cafés. They stretch east for over 4km (2.5 miles), interrupted only by the Port Olímpic, and finish at the Platja Nova Mar Bella.

Barcelona has some superb, if somewhat crowded, city beaches.

From the statue of Columbus, the **Moll de la Fusta** (NY), not so long ago the home of tatty crumbling warehouses, is now lined with fashionable restaurants – look for **Gambrinus** topped with a giant fibre-glass

lobster – and leads to the **Palau de Mar**, a big pink warehouse building sympathetically restored to house Barcelona's latest history museum, the **Museu d'Història de Catalunya** (Historical Museum of Catalonia). What it lacks in original exhibits it more than makes up for with the latest museum technology involving hundreds of inventive displays, including many hands-on exhibits. It is particularly good on recent history, so skim the early stuff if fatigue starts to set in.

Just east of here is the **Port Olímpic**, created for the Olympic yachting events and marked by the twin 150m (493ft)-high peaks of the Mapfre Tower (offices) and the Hotel Arts Barcelona. The **view★** from the top floors of the latter is stunning (*open only to guests*). The marina is full of yachts and

The Moll de la Fusta has been renovated to provide attractive waterside walks and an area of pleasant restaurants and cafés.

around it has sprung up one of the city's liveliest eating, drinking and clubbing zones, with international flagship establishments such as Planet Hollywood and the Baja Beach Club attracting the city's wealthy 18-to-40 crowd in their droves.

Parc de la Ciutadella★

Just set back from the waterfront, the **Ciutadella Park★** (DS) takes its name from a huge fortress (*ciutadella*) that was built here after Barcelona's defeat in 1714. It first intimidated then brooded over the city for over 150 years, before it was demolished and its grounds laid out as a park. In 1888 this was chosen as the site of the Universal Exhibition, from which several buildings still remain, and in 1892 one-third of it was given

The modern development of the Port Olímpic comes alive at night, when crowds arrive to take their pick from the endless range of places to eat, drink and go clubbing.

over to the **Parc Zoològic★** (Zoological Park). Open daily, this is hugely popular with local families, and though many of the cages and enclosures are small, the area is well landscaped. The Madagascar Jungle is a clever new exhibit and the Dolphin Show is a great draw, but the star of the zoo is undoubtedly Snowflake, the world's only captive white gorilla, and a real showman to boot.

Over the last century, the park has become one of the city's favourite places; indeed, for many years it was the only real park. Today it is filled with beautiful flowers,

The Zoological Parc's most truculent resident, Snowflake, a rare white gorilla.

Designed by the modernist Josep Vilaseca in Mudéjar style, the Arc de Triomf marked in grand style the entrance to the 1888 Universal Exhibition.

mature trees, water features (including a boating lake and a splendid cascade) and some delightful statuary. Bright green parrots flit noisily between the palms and take you a world away from the city's throbbing main roads.

The less-used northern entrance to the park is the grandest. Featuring the huge **Arc de Triomf** (Triumphal Arch), it was built for the Universal Exhibition and is decorated with ceramic figures. The park's other notable Exhibition building, just inside the northern gate, is the handsome red-brick neo-Gothic **Castell dels Tres Dragons★★** (Castle of the Three Dragons), designed by Domènech i Montaner as a café-restaurant. It now houses the **Museu de Zoologia★** (Zoology Museum) which is, for the most part, a relentlessly old-fashioned collection of stuffed creatures in glass cases. Nearby are

Water-spitting dragons, horses, chariots and cherubs adorn the Baroque cascade in Ciutadella Park.

the **Hivernacle** and the **Umbracle**, a greenhouse and conservatory with a bar attached, and the worthy but dull **Museu Martorell de Geologia** (Geology Museum).

In the north-east corner of the park is **La Cascada**, a glorious, over-the-top Baroque production of statuary, waterfalls and fountains which regularly spring into action. The young Gaudí assisted in its completion. There is a popular **boating lake** close by, and behind this beautiful formal gardens. To the east side the old arsenal building, the only surviving part of the original fortress, is

shared by the **Parlament de Catalunya**
(Catalan Parliament) and the **Museu d'Art
Modern** (Museum of Modern Art), not
really a museum of modern art at all as it
actually comprises work from the mid-19C to
the 1930s. The quality of exhibits is very
high, however, and the furniture and
decorative pieces from the *Modernisme*
period are particularly enjoyable.

MONTJUÏC★

From the seafront, **Montjuïc★** (BCT) (the
Mountain of the Jews) rises steeply above the
west of the city with its funfair rides invitingly
visible. By contrast, immediately below this is
the castle, a symbol of fear and repression
under the Franco regime. Beyond, at the top
of the hill, is the **Anella Olímpica★** (Olympic
Ring), built for the 1992 jamboree. On the
northern side of the hill is a clutch of
fascinating buildings designed for the
International Exhibition of 1929. Add to this
breathtaking **views** and two of Barcelona's
finest ancient and modern art collections
and you have two full days of exploring.

The West Slope of Montjuïc

The most direct public transport approach is
via the **funicular** which runs from Paral.lel
metro station (*note that it does not start until
11am*). Just by the terminus the **telefèric** (a
small, open, four-seat cable-car) makes the
short but very spectacular trip to the **Parc
d'atraccions** (*funfair open late-June to mid-
September, Tuesday to Saturday 5.30pm until
late, Sunday 11.30am until 11.15pm; rest of year
weekends only 11.30am to 10pm*).

The fair makes an enjoyable excursion,
with traditional and white-knuckle rides, but
a compelling reason for coming here is the

*Loop-the-loop, if you
dare, at Montjuïc's
funfair.*

fabulous **view** over the city below. This same perspective thrilled millions of television viewers during the 1992 Olympics high-diving championship. The pool, the **Piscina de Montjuïc**, is just below the funicular terminus and is now open for public swimming. Just by the funfair entrance is **Plaça Sardana**, where a charming statue immortalizes the Catalan *sardana* dance (*see* p.19). To the right of this is the **Plaça Mirador**, with wonderful views of the port.

Reboard the cable-car (the views just keep on getting better) for the short trip down to the **Castell de Montjuïc** (Montjuïc Castle). Built in the 18C, it was seized by Franco's troops and it was here in 1940 they executed Lluís Companys, the head of the Generalitat (Catalan government). Today it houses the **Museu Militar** (Military Museum), which features a comprehensive and extensive

Josep Canyas' evocative statue celebrates the traditional sardana.

Above: A table with a view, Montjuïc.

Below: Sculpture at the Fundació Miró.

collection of armour and arms from the 16C to the 20C. The castle roof and terraces offer more great **views** of the port. Take the cable-car back to the terminus or, alternatively, walk the short distance downhill to Plaça Armada from where the much larger **Transbordador Aeri** (covered cable-car) sweeps down to the seafront (*see* p.48).

A short walk from the terminus leads to the **Fundació Miró★★★** (Joan Miró Foundation). This gleaming white building houses the very best works of the internationally acclaimed Barcelona-born artist and sculptor Joan Miró (1893-1983), plus a limited selection of the work of some of his contemporaries. Miró's abstract, childlike doodle style is familiar to many through the Spanish Tourist Board logo and other symbols used commercially. One piece not to miss is the intriguing **Mercury Fountain★** by Alexander Calder. There is a lovely patio café here, too. Just below the Foundation are two minor museums, the

57

The Olympic Stadium during one of its quieter moments.

Museu Arqueològic★ (Archaeological Museum) and the **Museu Etnològic** (Ethnological Museum).

The **Estadi Olímpic★** (Olympic Stadium), the focus of the Games in 1992, is open to visitors (*guided tours by appointment; entrance on Avinguda Estadi*), with its **Galeria Olímpica** at the far end of the stadium. Here you can see medals, photographs, memorabilia and television pictures of some of the greatest moments of the 25th Olympiad. Almost adjacent is the **Palau Sant Jordi★★** sports and concert hall (*open only for events*), more Olympic swimming pools (*open to the public*) and the **Plaça de Europa**, which offers a different but still very impressive panorama of the city. The huge, white, space-age needle which dominates this part of the hill is a telecommunications tower.

The North Slope of Montjuïc

The northern approach to Montjuïc was initially designed to impress the world at the 1929 International Exhibition, and some 70 years on it is still one of the city's finest sights. It starts at the **Plaça d'Espanya** (BT), with its monumental **fountain** and statuary topped with a crucible that on summer nights is lit with an Olympic-style flame. It then passes through twin 47m (155ft)-high towers based on the Campanile di San Marco in Venice, to the Avinguda Reina Maria Cristina. This is lined with more fountains and pavilions built in 1929, restored in 1992, and now used on a daily basis by the many trade fairs which

Behind the grandiose fountain in Plaça d'Espanya are the twin obelisks marking the original entrance to the 1929 International Exhibition.

59

During the summer months the sound and light extravaganza at the National Palace attracts huge crowds.

Barcelona hosts. Among these is the minimalist **Pavelló Mies van der Rohe★★** (Mies van der Rohe Pavilion), acclaimed as one of the seminal examples of modern architecture in the world.

The long climb up the hill, via several flights of steps and elevators, is broken halfway by the huge **Font Màgica** (Magic Fountain). The spectacle of thousands of gallons of illuminated water dancing to Freddy Mercury and Montserrat Caballé's anthemic *Barcelona*, while laser beams stripe the sky behind the floodlit Palau Nacional (*see below*), will send a shiver down your spine. (*Water, light and music performances are usually given from June to September, Thursday to Sunday 9.45pm-11.45pm, but confirm with the tourist office.*)

At the very top is the **Palau Nacional**, a mock-Baroque palace built as a centrepiece to house the Spanish Pavilion at the International Exhibition in 1929 and now home to the **Museu Nacional d'Art de Catalunya**★★★ (National Museum of Catalonian Art), better-known as MNAC. This is generally held to be the city's most valuable treasure-trove and splits into two distinct parts, the **Romanesque Collection**★★★ and the **Gothic Collection**★★★. The Romanesque (11-13C) part is unique, largely comprising dozens of wall and apse frescoes, painstakingly

By day, the National Palace takes on a more serene beauty.

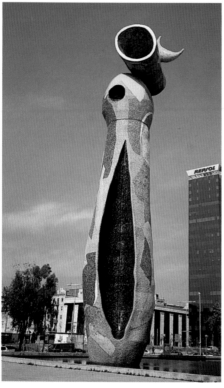

Miró's Dona i Ocell (Woman with Bird) sculpture is the centrepiece of Miró Park, close to Plaça d'Espanya.

removed from tiny, crumbling rural churches in the Catalan Pyrenees in order to save them from destruction or sale abroad. Many are reproduced here *in situ*; a video shows the process of removal and is worth seeing before you begin viewing the collection. The Gothic Collection is one of the best of its kind in the world, with 20 rooms filled with religious paintings of the highest quality, and some superb altar fronts

(the forerunners of retables). For a bit of light relief, visit the temporary section downstairs which deals with later periods and invariably features the works of world-famous artists. The museum is constantly expanding and by the turn of the millennium, if not before, will have added a major section on 16C-17C art.

To the west of the Palau Nacional is another 1929 survivor, the **Poble Espanyol★** (Spanish Village), described in its own literature as 'an architectural synopsis' (*open daily*). Here you wander through 17 different regions of reconstructed Spain, from Ávila to Zaragoza, and en route sample a little of their building styles, food, handicrafts and perhaps folk displays. It's all presented very professionally and in recent years has been spiced up by a lively clutch of nightclubs, spearheaded by the Torres de Ávila. Aim to get here in the early evening

Another remnant of the 1929 International Exhibition, the Poble Espanyol recreates the country's different architectural styles, customs and crafts.

for some shopping, a romantic ramble through the streets, a taste of Spanish regional cuisine, perhaps a flamenco show, then on to a nightclub.

EIXAMPLE★★

Eixample means extension, referring to the city's enlargement northwards between the 1860s and the 1920s. As this period coincided with the flowering of the *Modernisme* movement (*see* p.22) it holds some of the city's best examples of this fascinating architectural style. The most famous of these cluster conveniently along the **Passeig de Gràcia★★** (CS), a short walk north of Plaça de Catalunya.

The first three buildings of note are in a block known as the **Manzana de la Discordia★★** (the Block of Discord), which simply means that no two are alike. Walking from south to north, No 35 is the **Casa Lleó i Morera★**, by Domènech i Montaner (*open daily*), distinguished by its semi-circular balconies; No 41 is the **Casa Amatller★**, by Puig i Cadafalch, with coloured ceramics and a stepped gable reflecting the architect's

A Flemish stepped gable and coloured tiles decorate the façade of the Casa Amatller.

Low Countries influence (*open Thursday 10am-noon*). Best of all is the **Casa Batlló**★★ at No 43, a fairy-tale Gaudí creation with a scaly reptilian-like roof and mask-shaped balconies (*open Monday-Friday 10am-1pm*).

Gaudí's Casa Batlló, inspired by George and the Dragon.

65

*The fluid, curving
lines of Casa Batlló
are continued
through the
doorway and into
the building.*

Just a few metres around the corner from here, on Carrer d'Aragó, is the **Casa Montaner i Simón★**, one of the very first *Modernisme* buildings, designed in 1880 by Domènech i Montaner. It is now the home of the **Fundació Antoni Tàpies★★** (Tàpies Foundation), devoted to the works of the influential Barcelona-born abstract artist, Antoni Tàpies. His famous work *Cloud and Chair*, the maze-like jumble of tubing and wires on the roof, is an indication of the experimental abstract pieces by Tàpies on display inside, which are guaranteed to provoke controversy.

Return to the Passeig de Gràcia and after two more blocks north you will see on the

Ventilators on the roof of Casa Milà take on weird and wonderful forms.

left **Casa Milà★★★**, better known as **La Pedrera** (the Rock Quarry), built 1905-1911. This is recognised as Gaudí's finest secular building. Before you climb up to the roof to see the famous fantasy world of petrified soft ice-cream swirls and ventilators resembling medieval masked warriors, spend some time in the newly created **Espai Gaudí** (literally, Gaudí Space), in the attic of the building. This is an excellent exhibition on the man, his work and his methods, and is the perfect starting point for students of Gaudí and *Modernisme* (*see* p.22). On Friday and Saturday nights, from 9pm to midnight, you can visit the roof by moonlight and enjoy a drink up there. Night-time is also the best

67

Begun in 1882, La Sagrada Familia is still not completed some 100 years later, as the cranes testify.

time to see the Casa Battló (*see above*) when floodlights give it an even more bizarre appearance.

Close by on Avinguda Diagonal are two other *modernista* landmarks, both by Puig i Cadafalch. The **Casa Quadras** (at No 373)

has an impressive and rather sinister neo-Gothic façade and houses the **Museu Municipal de la Música** (Music Museum), with a display of instruments dating back to the 16C. By contrast, diagonally opposite, the **Casa Terrades★**, better-known as the **Casa de les Punxes** (House of Spikes), resembles more a north European château with a cheerful red tower (*no public entry*).

Undoubtedly the greatest building in the Eixample is **La Sagrada Família★★★** (CR) (Church of the Holy Family), the enigmatic church which has become an emblem of the city and one of Spain's principal landmarks. It was begun in 1882 as the project of Francesco de P Villar, but by 1883 it already belonged to Gaudí. Its basic design is rooted firmly in the city's Gothic tradition, but there familiarity ends. Stonework which 'drips' like melted candle wax, towers which resemble perforated cigars that rocket 100m (328ft) into the heavens, sculptures of nature and broken-ceramic mosaic decorations are all part of this visual feast.

The **Nativity Façade★★**, surmounted by the great towers, is a storybook in itself, with numerous biblical scenes sculpted on its walls. A pair of binoculars is useful to pick out the details – the flight from Egypt, the three wise men and the shepherds, the Angel Gabriel and Christ's family tree. To get a real feel for the building's scale and detail take the lift as far as possible (it ascends 60m/197ft), walk up the rest of the way, enjoy the panoramic **view★★**, then walk the whole way back down. Although the climb is most impressive, it is not recommended for those who do not like heights – the narrow, winding stairs, with glimpses of the outside, make some people

Vivid blue stained-glass windows are set into the intricately carved stonework of La Sagrada Família.

feel very dizzy. The church is unfinished and as Gaudí did not leave detailed plans there is inevitably controversy about how it should be completed. Fittingly, Gaudí is buried here, in the **crypt** (*open during services only*) with a small museum exhibition housed nearby (*open daily*).

OTHER ATTRACTIONS

Tibidabo

On a hot summer weekend evening there's only one place to be in Barcelona, and that is the hill of Tibidabo (AR). Its views, cool air and so-called **Muntanya Magic** (Magic Mountain) funfair deservedly draw Barcelonans by the thousand.

Getting to the city's northernmost tourist attraction can be an adventure in itself. The direct route to the funfair is via the special **Tibibús**, which runs every weekend and

Tuesday to Sunday in July and August from Plaça de Catalunya. Alternatively, take the FF.CC metro line from Plaça de Catalunya to Avinguda de Tibidabo (note that owing to long-term underground construction works the service may end at the stop before this, El Putget, in which case a bus will take you on the last leg). At Avinguda de Tibidabo, the famous **Tramvia Blau** (Blue Tramway) will be waiting to take you up to the foot of Tibidabo. This is a splendid service, utilizing original turn-of-the-century tram cars with

Tibidabo's famous Blue Tramway makes light work of a very steep climb.

In addition to the thrills of the rides, Tibidabo's funfair provides outstanding views across the city.

polished wooden seats and shiny brass fitments. Confusingly, they are not all blue and on winter weekdays an ordinary bus service replaces the trams.

On the way up you will see the **Museu de la Ciència** (Museum of Science) – quite unmistakable as it has a submarine outside. Inside is full of interesting hands-on exhibits. At the Tramvia terminus the **Funicular de Tibidabo** covers the last leg of the journey, depositing you right outside the

Parc d'atraccions (funfair). Sprawling down the hill, lushly landscaped and divided into several themed areas, this is an excellent evening out for all the family, with a good mixture of thrills for teenagers and gentle rides for youngsters, plus shows and special attractions such as the fascinating **Museu d'Automates** and the terrifying **Krueger Hotel**. The former features a collection of historic automatons from all over the world, while the latter is a haunted-house-style

A model fascinates youngsters at the Tibidabo funfair Museu d'Automates.

attraction starring Freddy *Nightmare on Elm Street* Krueger, which aims to scare you witless (not recommended for young children!).

The church immediately above the funfair, the **Sagrat Cor**, is worth visiting in its own right, but the **views★★** it offers are spellbinding. Start by going up in the lift which takes you to a terrace 542m (1 778ft) above sea-level. You must then walk up narrow winding stone steps for the final 26m (85ft) to stand immediately below the statue of Jesus, where the wind blows hard and the 360° views are unsurpassable. On a clear day, you can see inland to the Pyrenees and Montserrat and as far out to sea as Mallorca, or so they say. If you still haven't had enough of the high life, there's one last viewing option. Take the free shuttle train which runs from below the church to the giant **Torre de Collserola**. Here you board a glass lift which whisks you up the outside of this massive telecommunications tower to a glazed viewing gallery at 560m (1 837ft; *closed Monday and Tuesday*).

Parc Güell★★

This splendid landscaped park (BR) (*open daily*) was Gaudí's final secular project and is certainly one of his most popular creations. His signature fairy-tale spires and roofs mark several buildings, but one of the most striking features is the great bank of winding, swirling **benches★★**, garishly decorated with broken ceramics which are set on a look-out point over the city. Parc Güell was originally conceived as a housing estate to include 60 houses, and the famous **Hall of Columns** (below the benches) was designed as market colonnades; sadly, the project was never realised. The park also

A mosaic-covered roof and spiralling tower rise up from Gaudí's unfinished housing estate, Parc Güell.

includes the enjoyable **Casa Museu Gaudí** (*closed Saturday*) where the great man lived for much of his last 20 years.

Pedralbes
Originally a country village where monks and kings retreated from the city, Pedralbes [AS] has now been fully absorbed into the suburbs of Barcelona. However, the **Monestir de Pedralbes★★** (Pedralbes Monastery) is still a wonderful place in which to escape the city bustle. Hidden

The famous 'wave benches' surrounding the main square of Parc Güell are a popular meeting place for locals at weekends.

behind high gated walls, it is a peaceful self-contained community and its fabric is one of the best-preserved in Europe. Here, more than at Montserrat (*see* p.80), or at any of the other famous Catalan monasteries, you get a sense of the day-to-day life of such an institution. The 14C **cloister**★, which is a magnificent example of Catalan-Gothic architecture, comprises three storeys and you can peep into many of the original **cells** where the devotees of the Clarissan order spent their daily lives (a small number of nuns are still resident). The kitchens, infirmary, refectory, a valuable **frescoed chapel**★★★ and the chapter-room are also open to view. For most art lovers, the jewel in the crown is the **Col·lecció Thyssen-Bornemisza** (Thyssen-Bornemisza Collection) which occupies a wing of the monastery. This consists of 72 paintings and eight sculptures of the very highest order (including works by Lucas Cranach, Titian, Veronese, Tiépolo, Tintoretto and Canaletto), mostly representing Italian art from the Middle Ages to the 18C. Finally, do not miss the **church**★, where the monastery's founder, Queen Elisenda de Montcada, lies in a splendid tomb.

Less striking but still of interest is the **Palau de Pedralbes** (Royal Palace of Pedralbes), a 15-minute walk or a five-minute bus ride away. Modest by palace standards, it was built in Italianate style in 1919-1929 for Alfonso XIII onto an existing building which was formerly the home of Gaudí's patron, Eusebi Güell. Its public rooms are now devoted to two museum collections. The **Museu de Ceràmica**★ (Ceramics Museum) is probably of less interest to the average visitor than the

Museu de les Arts Decoratives (Museum of Decorative Arts), a journey through the world of interior design from the Middle Ages to the present, with some startling modern pieces in stark juxtaposition to their palace setting.

For something completely different, make the short journey across the Avinguda Diagonal to the **Stadion Camp Nou**, home of the world-famous Barcelona Football Club (*see* p.109). You can peer down onto the magnificent stadium which regularly

Step back in time as you wander through the peaceful 14C cloisters of Pedralbes Monastery.

Football fever is a way of life in Barcelona.

holds 120 000 fervent fans, then enter the **Museu del Futbol Club de Barcelona**. A series of displays (photographs and memorabilia) is dedicated to each era of the club's history since its foundation in 1899, while a multi-bank video screen looks at recent club highlights. It's a very popular place of pilgrimage for football fans from all over the world, and the official *Barça* shop by the entrance is invariably packed (there are others in town).

EXCURSIONS FROM BARCELONA

A car is not necessary for any of the following excursions; driving in and out of Barcelona is no pleasure, and all are easily accessible by rail.

Montserrat**

40km (25 miles) north-west of Barcelona
The spiritual heart of Catalunya and the second-most important shrine in all Spain after Santiago de Compostela, Montserrat draws around a million pilgrims each year to venerate **La Moreneta**** (the Little Dark Madonna or Black Virgin). According to legend, St Luke himself carved the figure and, shortly after the death of Christ, St Peter brought it to Barcelona where she was adopted as the region's patron saint. The icon has been at Montserrat since early medieval times, when one of the many hermitages scattered across this hilly area was enlarged to become the original monastery. This was largely destroyed in 1811 by Napoleon's troops, though La Moreneta was spirited to safety, and the present building dates from 1874.

At first sight the huge, square, pink-brick complex looks more like Fort Knox than a place of worship. Home to around 300 brothers, it is very much a working monastery; visitors are admitted only to the 16C basilica, which houses La Moreneta and where the faithful join long queues to file past and fleetingly touch the statue. Try to be here at 1pm when the world-famous **Escolanía boys' choir** sings. There is also an interesting **museum** which reflects the great wealth of the monastery, including materials from the lands of the Bible, works from

A dramatic cable-car ride is the best way to appreciate the breathtaking setting of Montserrat Monastery.

modern artists such as Picasso and Dalí, and Old Masters paintings by the likes of El Greco and Caravaggio. The museum is divided into two, the older section being located next to a beautiful late 15C Gothic cloister.

For the average overseas visitor (not here on pilgrimage) the great attraction of Montserrat, which means saw-tooth mountain, is its dramatic **physical setting★★★**. The best approach is by cable-car, the Telefèric de Montserrat Aeri, which is linked directly to Barcelona (Plaça d'Espanya) by the FF.CC railway. The cable-car soars up over 1 000m (3 289ft), often breaking through the clouds into the sunshine on the mountain top. After visiting the monastery, try some of the famous *mel i mató* (honey and curd cheese) sold by stallholders just outside the main gates, then take one (or both) of the funicular rides which penetrate the mountains. The **Funicular de Sant Joan** offers the classic picture-postcard view down onto the monastery but the **views★** from Sant Cova are also magnificent, and from both stations there are beautiful signposted **walks** of varying lengths leading to a number of ancient hermitages.

Sitges★★
40km (25 miles) south of Barcelona
By far the best resort on the Costa Daurada, **Sitges★★** is attractive, fashionable, vibrant and largely unspoilt by the excesses of 20C seaside tourism. It is the Barcelonans' favourite weekend retreat, so be prepared for crowds on the beaches and in town (book accommodation well ahead), and traffic jams which reach nightmare

Fashionable, yet unspoilt, Sitges has fine beaches and an attractive old town quarter.

proportions – it's much easier to take the train.

The town's **beaches** are excellent and stretch either side of the *punta*, the headland topped by the landmark parish church which is a great sight when floodlit by night. Behind this is the **old town★★**, a maze of narrow cobbled streets, and the romantically named **Palau Maricel** (the Palace of Sea and Sky). Looking for all the

Blue ceramic tiling and lush greenery create a cool, refreshing courtyard in Palau Maricel.

world like a cleaned-up medieval palace, it was actually built in the 1920s for the American businessman and art lover, Charles Deering. Inside, in a glorious setting with full-length floor-to-ceiling windows looking straight out to sea, the **Museu Maricel de Mar★** houses part of Deering's collection of art, the collection of Perez Rosales and various objects from around the world.

Next door, the **Museu del Cau Ferrat★★** (literally, Museum of the Iron Lair) was the

Sitges has a maze of narrow cobbled streets for the visitor to explore at leisure.

home and workshop of the painter and writer, Santiago Rusiñol (1861-1931). Like Gaudí, he was a brilliant wrought-ironworker and exponent of *Modernisme*: his meetings here with fellow artists first established Sitges as a fashionable artists' and intellectuals' colony. In addition to Rusiñol's works, there are some glorious ceramics and crystals, and paintings by such luminaries as El Greco and Picasso, which all contribute to make this one of Spain's best small museums. A third collection worth seeking out in town is the **Museu Romàntic**, housed in the **Casa Llopis★**, a lavishly decorated 19C mansion full of fascinating period objects and a famous collection of dolls.

Above all, Sitges is famous for its **Carnaval** celebrations (*see* p.88-89), a time when the whole town seems to go crazy and its sizeable gay population really let their hair down.

The Wine Region
55km (34 miles) west of Barcelona
Vilafranca del Penedès★ is the capital of the
Alt Penedès wine region, and its excellent
Museu de Vilafranca/Museu del Vino★
(Museum of Wine) makes a logical starting
point for any wine tour. The museum is
located in Vilafranca's very own Barri Gòtic
(Gothic Quarter), in a beautiful building
which was a former palace of the Counts of
Barcelona. Dioramas illustrate how wine has
been produced throughout the ages, and
huge 2 000-year-old wooden wine presses are
reminders that this was the favourite drink
of the Romans. At the end of your visit you
can sample the local wines in a re-creation of
an 18C *bodega* (tavern).

Vilafranca is at its liveliest on a Saturday,
when it hosts one of the region's most
colourful general markets. Stroll along its
leafy main avenues, the Rambla Sant
Francesc and the Rambla Nostra Senyora,
and pay a visit to the late-medieval Basílica
de Santa María, the adjacent Palau Baltà and
the **Sant Francesc Convent★**.

Just outside the town are the vineyards of
Torres, king of Catalan wines, and
undisputedly one of the world's great
winemakers. Torres are known for their
technological prowess and innovation, and
tours reflect this preoccupation. Keen
oenologists and fans of stainless steel may
enjoy it, but more romantically inclined
wine lovers should head 10km (6 miles)
north-east to **Sant Sadurní d'Anoia**, the
Capital del Cava.

Cava, the 'Catalan Champagne', is
produced by over 20 manufacturers in Sant
Sadurní, though few visitors venture further
than the premises of **Freixenet**, located

conveniently near the railway station. Tours of the cellars are conducted free of charge by friendly, knowledgeable guides. The town's other internationally renowned producer is **Codorniu**, who also conduct tours of their **cellars**★ and are famous for their *modernista* buildings designed by Puig i Cadafalch.

Wine tours are generally conducted at regular intervals on weekdays (with a gap for lunch) and on Saturday mornings. Enquire at the tourist office in Vilafranca del Penedès or contact the *bodegas* direct: Freixenet ☎ 818 32 00; Codoniu ☎ 818 32 32.

Proving that the traditional methods of wine-making are still alive and well at a wine festival.

WEATHER

Barcelona is at its best in late spring to early summer (late April to early June) and late summer (September), when temperatures still exceed 20°C (68°F), and there are cool Mediterranean breezes. In late July and most of August the heat becomes very oppressive, with high humidity and temperatures in the mid-30°C (over 90°C) range; air-conditioned accommodation is essential for a good night's sleep. Winters are wet but mild by north European standards (the average temperature in December and January is around 12°C/53°F). March and October/November are the wettest months, with an average rainfall of 85mm (3.5in), and November through to March experience a more modest average of 42mm (2in). The summer months are usually dry.

CALENDAR OF EVENTS

There are said to be over 140 different festivals going on in Barcelona each year. The following are the main celebrations:

5, 6 January: Epiphany (*Festa del Reis*), the Procession of the Three Wise Men through the city starts the year's festivities.

17 January: *Festa de Els tres tombs.*

February: International Vintage Car Rally, from Sitges to Barcelona.

February/March week before Lent: Carnival (*Carnaval*), with costumed celebrations and parades. The best (certainly the most outrageous) are in Sitges.

23 April: St George's Day (*Dia de Sant Jordi*), particularly colourful on La Rambla; men present women with a rose, and women give a book to men and there are stalls selling these all over the city.

Corpus Christi: *Líou com balla* (meaning 'the egg that dances'), an egg is put on the water fountain in the cloister of the cathedral and it 'dances' during the whole day, without breaking.

23 June: St John's Day (*Dia de Sant Joan*), noisy summer solstice evening celebrations, with general festivities, culminating in massive bonfires and firework displays on Montjuïc and Tibidabo.

24 June: *La Verbena de Sant Joan.*

One of the biggest and liveliest carnivals is held in Sitges.

Of dragons, giants and human castles...

Not content with the usual singing, dancing and fireworks associated with a typical Spanish *fiesta*, the Catalans have invented their own exuberant and individual forms of merry-making. The most distinctive and spectacular are *castellers*, men and boys who climb on to each other's shoulders to form daring and precarious **human towers** which can reach up to seven storeys. These can be seen at the Festa de la Mercé and at the Festa Major in Vilafranca del Penedès (end August/ beginning September).

Catalonian **dragons** are a more common sight, either large specimens constructed from wood and canvas, or smaller papier-mâché creatures which, like their mythical ancestors, should not be approached on account of their penchant for spitting fire. Controlled by one or two revellers, they career madly through the streets, pausing only to refill their mouths with fireworks,

and then spin like dervishes, sending the watching crowd yelping and flying in all directions. It can be quite disarming so stand well back, guard your eyes and be watchful with small children.

By contrast are the gentle *gegants* (giants) paraded at local *festa majors* (village or district festivals) and at Barcelona's Festa de la Mercé. These too are papier-mâché creations – based on ancient kings and queens or lords and ladies – which tower up to 4.5m (15ft) high, and are controlled by operators who peep out from between the figures' skirts. They are often accompanied by *capgrosses* (literally, 'big heads'), grotesque caricature figures with large silly fixed grins.

Fiery dragon, Festa de la Mercé.

June–July: Grec Summer Festival, a festival of national and international dance, theatre and music at various venues throughout the city, including the Teatre Grec (Greek Theatre) on Montjuïc.

Week of 24 September: *Festa de la Mercé* (Feast of Our Lady of Mercy) is the city's main festival, with three to four days of street celebrations, including *gegants, castellers, dracs* and a wonderful firework display.

October: Jazz festival in the Ciutat Vella.

24 December: *Missa del Gall* is celebrated in all churches.

In Sitges:

26 June: San Bartolomé Day, when people dance the *moixiganga* with *gegants* and capgrosses.

October: *Festival Internacional de Cinema de Catalunya.*

ACCOMMODATION

As in most European cities, there is no shortage of accommodation in Barcelona, ranging from luxurious and very expensive hotels to basic stop-overs. Older hotels are concentrated along Las Ramblas, and the Eixample area has a good selection of mid-priced hotels. The best area for cheaper accommodation is the old Gothic Quarter.

Hostales (marked Hs) and *hostal-residencias* (HsR), both range from one to three stars and offer reasonable en-suite or private facilities.

Hoteles (H) are graded from one to five stars, with a one-star hotel costing about the same as three-star *hostales,* but as you go up the scale the levels of luxury and pricing increase considerably.

The following prices are a guide to what

you can expect to pay for a double room, per night, with breakfast:

    5 star: over 25 000 ptas
    4 star: 15 000-25 000
    3 star: 12 000-20 000
    2 star: 8 000-12 000
    1 star: under 10 000

The Michelin *Red Guide España-Portugal* lists accommodation and restaurants in Barcelona and the surrounding area.

Details of youth hostels and other accommodation for students and young people are provided by REAJ, Calle Ortega y Gasset 71, 28006 Madrid; ☎ (93) 347 76 31.

Recommendations

Ciutat Vella

15 000- 25 000

G H Barcino (Jaume 1-6, 08002 Barcelona ☎ 302 20 12 Fax 301 42 42) Old, restored building in the Gothic neighbourhood.

12 000 - 20 000

Montecarlo (La Rambla 124, 08002 Barcelona ☎ 412 04 04 Fax 318 73 23) Historic building on Las Ramblas, entirely renovated. Spacious garage.

8 000 - 12 000

Lleó (Pelai 22, 08001 Barcelona ☎ 318 13 12 Fax 412 26 57) Located in the centre of town, recently renovated. Modern facilities.

Under 10 000

Cortés (Santa Ana 25, 08002 Barcelona ☎ 317 91 12 Fax 302 78 70) Simple hotel, acceptably comfortable, moderate prices; situated near the Plaça de Catalunya (therefore some of the rooms may not always be very peaceful).

On Diagonal

Over 25 000

Claris (Pau Claris 150, 08009 Barcelona

☎ 487 62 62 Fax 215 79 70) Modern facilities along with antiques and an archaeological museum. The period furnishings are stylish, the ambience top flight.

Condes de Barcelona (Passeig de Gràcia 75, 08008 Barcelona ☎ 488 22 00 Fax 487 14 42) Historic building in the city's 'Golden Quarter'.

N H Calderón (Rambla de Catalunya 26, 08007 Barcelona ☎ 301 00 00 Fax 317 31 57) Business clientele. The restaurant is well-known and luxurious. Modern facilities.

Gran Derby (Loreto 28, 08029 Barcelona ☎ 322 20 62 Fax 419 68 20) The decor is lush with green plants and pretty interior patios. Unusual rooms, some on two levels.

12 000 - 20 000

Regina (Bergara 2, 08002 Barcelona ☎ 301 32 32 Fax 318 23 26) Located in the centre. Very spacious rooms.

Catalunya Plaza (Plaça de Catalunya 7, 08002 Barcelona ☎ 317 71 71 Fax 317 78 55) Old, renovated building. Moderately comfortable.

Antibes (Carrer Diputació 394 ☎ 232 62 11) Popular with travelling sales reps, recently renovated. Family atmosphere. Spacious garage.

Under 10 000

L'Alguer (Passatge Pere Rodriguez 20, 08028 Barcelona ☎ 334 60 50 Fax 333 83 65) Modest and simple, just acceptably comfortable; priced accordingly.

FOOD AND DRINK

Catalan cuisine is not easy to define, and 'typical Barcelona food' is an even more elusive concept because of the city's cosmopolitan nature.

A seafood feast.

Main Dishes

Pick up a menu from most typical
restaurants, however, and you'll see **grilled
meats** and **game** (the simple but robust taste
of the Catalan countryside), **rice dishes**
(from the paddy-fields of the Ebro Delta and
the influence of Valencia) and, of course,
fish and **shellfish**. Add the ubiquitous sauce-
based ingredients of garlic, olive oil, ripe
tomatoes, red peppers, onions and a few
herbs, stir, and things are beginning to take
shape. Often garlic and olive oil are

95

A traditionally-cooked seafood paella.

combined to make *all i oli*, a creamy garlic sauce which makes a delicious simple accompaniment to grilled meat.

That most famous Spanish dish, **paella**, which mixes most of the above ingredients (rice, chicken, rabbit, seafood and so on), is often on the menu. An interesting local rice and seafood dish is *arròs negre* (literally, black rice), which is cooked in squid's ink. *Zarzuela* is a very rich tomato-based stew, with great quantities of any and every fish and seafood thrown in.

Merluza (hake), usually served *a la romana* (battered and deep-fried), is a national

standby and *bacallà/bacalao* (salt cod) in all
its many forms is a favourite over much of
Iberia. A common dish is *bacallà amb
samfaina*, served in a ratatouille-like sauce.
Another interesting variation is *esqueixada*, a
cold salad consisting of the fish (salt cod)
mixed with red pepper, onions, olives and
tomatoes. Don't confuse this with the
similar-sounding Catalan salad speciality
escalivada – grilled and peeled peppers,
onions and aubergines.

Butifarra is the local sausage – of the
English link variety (as opposed to the
salami slicing kind) – and is often served *con
mongetes*, with haricot beans, and is well
worth a try.

At lunchtimes many establishments offer a
special-price *menú del día*, a fixed-price menu
(usually three courses) with a limited choice
of dishes. Depending on the restaurant itself
and what is on the menu, this can be a
cheap but uninspiring option, or
alternatively it may offer a taste of a higher
class of cuisine at a bargain price. Certainly
it is worth considering.

Meal portions are almost always on the
large side in Catalonian restaurants, so it
may be best to skip the starter altogether.

Snacks
To taste the best local food, you can't beat
snacking in Barcelona. **Tapas**, small portions
of a whole range of foods, usually displayed
on the counter, is a Spanish institution
rather than a Catalan tradition, but there
are many fine *tapas* bars in the city. Prices
are usually reasonable but often not
displayed, so it's always best to ask first. A
small portion is a *pincho*, a large portion is a
*ració*n.

Los Caracoles tapas bar, off La Rambla, is a Barcelona institution, and worth a visit for its wonderful interior and fine food.

The most distinctive Catalan snack food is *pa amb tomaquet* (bread with tomato), made by simply rubbing garlic and a cut ripe tomato on to a sliced baguette, then drizzling with olive oil. Grill it and you have a *torrada*. Some bars specialise in *torradas*, adding seafood, hams and whatever else to make a filling snack.

Tapas bars should not be confused with café-bars, which also display restaurant-type food on the counter. A request for a *ración* here will generally result in a meal-sized portion, though these can be the best value of all. If in doubt, look and see what is on the locals' plates.

Desserts and Drinks

The ubiquitous dessert is *flan*, the Spanish *crème caramel*, often good because it is home-made. Better still is *crema catalana*, a deluxe-version of *flan*, flavoured with cinnamon and lemon and topped with a hard, glassy, caramelised crust.

Catalonia produces excellent still and sparkling **wines** and is home to three internationally famous marques: **Torres**, who produce many top-quality table wines, and the *cava bodegas* of **Freixenet** and **Codorniu**. **Cava** is Spain's answer to champagne, produced by the traditional *méthode champenoise* and consumed in vast quantities, by the glass and by the bottle, in the city's specialist *cava* bars (two of the best are listed below). You can go into any bar, however, and sample the local house wine (*vino de la casa*) by the glass. Sometimes it's excellent, sometimes it's not, but at least it *is* local and it never costs more than a few pesetas. In the heat of the summer, many locals drink *tinto de verano* (literally 'summer red'), a surprisingly pleasant cool mix of local red wine and *casera* (a lemonade-style drink).

Coffee is the national pick-me-up and after-dinner drink, either small and black (*café solo*), small with a dash of milk (*cortado*), or large and white (*café con leche,* or *café amb llet* in Catalan). An unusual summer cooler is *horchata/orxata*, a milky drink made from *chufa/xufa* (a type of nut).

Recommendations

Here are a few bars and restaurants (all moderately priced, except where indicated) which capture the spirit of eating and drinking in Barcelona. Telephone numbers are given only where reservations are accepted.

Restaurants

Set Portes (Passeig d'Isabel II ☎ 319 30 46) Elegant wood-panelled mid-19C city legend. Expensive.

Els Quatre Gats (Carrer Montsió 3 bis ☎ 302 41 40) Famous *modernista*-decorated haunt of Picasso, good for food or just a drink (closed August).

Los Caracoles (Carrer Escudellers 14 ☎ 302 31 85) A Barcelona landmark, just off La Rambla, with a beautiful traditional interior and flaming spit-roasted chicken outside.

La Garduña (Carrer Morera 17-19 ☎ 302 43 23) Charming two-storey warren behind La Boquería market, offering a good-value lunchtime *menú del día*.

Quinze Nits (Plaça Reial 6) An excellent place to get acquainted with traditional and especially new-wave Catalan food. Very popular; no reservations taken so arrive early to avoid queues.

Agut (Carrer Gignàs 16 ☎ 315 17 09) Popular with young people and regulars; very good value for money.

Can Lluís (Carrer La Cera 49 ☎ 441 60 81) Family cooking and atmosphere. Tables are sometimes shared between different customers. Good value for money.

La Fonda (Passatge Escudellers 10 ☎ 301 75 15) Youthful ambience. Very affordable.

Els Ocellets (Ronda de Sant Pau 55 ☎ 441

10 46) Very friendly and youthful
atmosphere; reasonable prices, unaffected
modern style.

Ca la María (Tallers 76 bis ☎ 318 89 93)
Good Catalan cooking; frequented by locals.

Pitarra (Avinyó 56 ☎ 301 16 47) Good value
menu del día; restaurant decorated with
souvenirs of the poet Pitarra.

Bar Celta (Carrer de la Mercé 16) One of
the city's best seafood *tapas* bars, with
excellent displays and prompt service.

Cava Bars

El Xampanyet (Carrer de Montcada 22)
Enjoy seafood *tapas* and *cava* in this blue-

*The Port Olímpic is
one of Barcelona's
liveliest areas for
eating and drinking.*

tiled city legend (closed August).
Cal Paixano (Carrer Reina Cristina 5 –
behind Set Portes) Hustle, bustle, loads of
atmosphere, good sandwiches and a choice
of *cavas* at ridiculously low prices.

Cafés-Bars

Bar del Pi (Plaça Sant Josep Oriol) The
position as much as the drinks and *tapas*
make this a must on a night's bar-hopping.
Mesón del Café (Carrer Llibreteria 16) Tiny,
long-established hole-in-the-wall place just
off Plaça Sant Jaume, with plenty of
character and delicious coffee and cakes.
Boadas (Carrer Taillers 1) Specialises in all
sorts of mixed drinks and cocktails. Friendly
atmosphere, lots of regular customers.

Good general locations for eating and
drinking include: the **Port Olímpic** and **Port
Vell** – for young trendy restaurants and bars;
Carrer de la Mercé – good *tapas* bars and
typical down-to-earth Galician cider and
cheese bars; **Carrer de Montcada** – relaxing
fashionable courtyard cafés and bars.

Designer Bars

A product of the slick 1980s, the Barcelona
bar moderno phenomenon is still going strong
and has bequeathed to the city some of the
most weird and wonderful drinking places
in Europe (many of these also double as
nightclubs). Characterised by hi-tech
interiors, high-fashion customers, high
priced drinks and often high-volume, high-
tempo music (when they also become
known as *bars musicals*), these are not places
for the faint-hearted or the budget traveller.
If you only visit one designer bar in
Barcelona, however, make it the **Torres de**

Ávila at the Poble Espanyol, which has become a nocturnal tourist sight in its own right (closed August). Its night-and-day themed architecture is stunning; in the main bar a huge eye on a film screen blinks continually and is mirrored in the glass floor on which you stand.

Less obviously attractive but equally popular are the heavy-duty, post-modern techno shrines, of which the most famous is the capacious **Nick Havanna's**, Carrer Rosselló 208. Also recommended is **Network**, Avinguda Diagonal 616, which borrows its décor from the film *Blade Runner*.

Less self-conscious and much more relaxed are the wacky theme bars also spawned by this movement. **La Fira**, Carrer Provença 171, where you can enjoy all the fun of the fair without going to Tibidabo or Montjuïc, is the pick of them. Also worth a look are the **Bosque de les Fades** (Fairies' Wood, *see* p.40) and **Dive**, a Steven Spielberg-designed submarine-style restaurant-bar in the Port Vell Maremagnum complex.

An antique shop in the Barri Gòtic.

SHOPPING

The joy of shopping in Barcelona is that most of its shops are small and individual. There are relatively few malls and only two department stores (both El Corte Inglés). What's more, the latest styles and old traditions co-exist happily – from dusty antiquarian and antique shops to hip interior design and street fashions. Specialisation is a Barcelona tradition, and in the old town there are many intriguing single-product stores selling *turron* (nougat), *bacallà/bacalao* (salt cod), feathers, cigars and candles, to name but a few.

For **antiques**, look in the Gothic Quarter, particularly around Carrer de la Palla. There is a market in Avinguda Catedral every Thursday. Look, too, in the Eixample around Carrer Dos de Maig and Carrer Consell de Cent. The latter also hosts Barcelona's best **flea market**, Els Encants (*open Mon, Wed, Fri and Sat*).

Fashion victims should bring their credit cards to the Passeig de Gràcia, Rambla de Catalunya, Diagonal and Plaça Francesc Macià. In the old town, Carrer Portaferrisa (off La Rambla) is another trendy (and cheaper) street for clothing. Continue along here to Avinguda Portal de l'Angel, another important general shopping street.

For good quality **souvenirs** (ceramics are always a good bet) look in individual museum shops. The BCN Original shop, next to the tourist office at Plaça Catalunya, pulls together the best of the museums' collections, and stocks other typical Barcelona items. The Poble Espanyol is also a convenient collection of crafts (Spanish, rather than just local) in one place, as are the stalls which set up at the bottom end of La Rambla on weekend afternoons and evenings.

If you cannot do without everything-under-one-roof shopping, try the eclectic **Maremagnum**, the 200-shop strong **Barcelona Glòries** on Avinguda Diagonal, or **El Corte Inglés** on Plaça Catalunya.

ENTERTAINMENT AND NIGHTLIFE

Barcelona has been famed for its nightlife, particularly its cutting-edge designer bars, for well over a decade. Now, with its emergence as an international holiday playground, new areas such as the **Port Olímpic** and **Port Vell** have developed to cater for all tastes.

The city's nightlife starts late and goes on well into the early hours; here, the Port Olímpic prepares for the night's revellers.

The city eats, drinks and parties late and long; many clubs don't get going until around 2am (or later) and are still grooving long after the sun rises. The difference between a bar and a club is slight; the latter generally stays open later and charges more. Be warned that Barcelona's trendier type of nightlife does not come cheap. The price of a beer can easily reach 1 000 pesetas, and admission prices are capricious, depending on your appearance, what time and day it is, what entertainment (if any) is on offer.

As a general rule, most first-time visitors stick to the areas mentioned above (although these too are also frequented by the locals). The **Poble Espanyol** is very popular, and not just for its legendary Torres de Ávila (*see* p.63). Two of the most famous and longest-established clubs are **Otto Zutz** (Carrer de Lincoln) and **Bikini** (Carrer Deu i Mata 105), but just pick up a copy of Barcelona's listings magazine, *La Guía del Ocio*, from any news-stand for dozens of other ideas.

A more sedate and much cheaper kind of evening entertainment can be found simply by strolling the main squares and streets of the old town on summer nights. Buskers and bands, often of very good quality, abound on and just off La Rambla, while watching the spectators is entertainment in itself. A trip to either of the **funfairs** at Tibidabo and Montjuïc is also recommended, for the magnificent views as much as the fairground rides. For a different kind of thrill, visit the **IMAX cinema** in the Port Vell (*see* p.48).

The performing arts are well represented in the city and a **classical music** concert at the **Palau de la Música Catalana** (*see* p.35) will be a highlight of any holiday. The

famous **Liceu** (*see* p.39), the traditional home of **opera** and **ballet**, will not be operational until the 1998-99 season, but there are alternative venues. The Centre d'Informació at the Palau de la Virreina, halfway along La Rambla, acts as an information point and a booking office for many live performances.

There are also several **jazz**, **rock** and **blues** outlets (see *La Guía del Ocio* for details, or the city's other main listing magazine, *La Agenda de Barcelona*).

Flamenco dancing is a southern tradition, but as there are a good number of

Street entertainment on La Rambla.

Busker in Parc Güell.

Andalucíans resident in Barcelona so authentic flamenco *tablaos* (nightspots) have followed them. **El Tablao de Carmen** (Poble Espanyol) is a long-standing favourite with both tourists and locals.

Barcelona has a good history of **music-hall** and **cabaret** – the most famous place in town is **El Molino**, its bawdy and camp revues somehow transcending language problems and striking an international chord.

SPORTS

In the heat of the summer the outdoor **swimming** pools on Montjuïc are excellent places to cool off, while the **Centre Municipal de Tennis** (at the end of the metro line at Vall d'Hebron), also built for the 1992 Games, has good courts, but no equipment for hire.

The best **golf** course is by the airport, Club de Golf El Prat, several times host to the Spanish Open. Winter weekends are reserved for club members only; to play at other times you must be a member of a recognised club at home.

Spectator Sports

As even the least committed non-football fan will notice, there is a blue-and-red striped omnipresence in the city that goes by the name of *Barça*, or, to give it its full name, the **Futbol Club de Barcelona**. *Barça* is, as the locals say, more than just a club. It is an industry (said to be the fifth most successful in Spain) with its logo on everything from sweets to underwear, a national (Catalan) identity and obsession, and the football club with the largest membership in the world, counting over 100 000 *socios* – among them the Pope! Given this huge popularity, and despite having a ground which holds 120 000 spectators, it is quite difficult to get hold of tickets for matches. Apply as far as possible in advance. If you are unlucky, you could try to watch the city's other first division team, RCD Espanyol, and there is always the *Barça* museum to visit.

Barça also have a first-class **basketball** team, also fanatically supported, so once again tickets are hard to come by. Look in *La Guía del Ocio*, the local press, or ask at your hotel for details.

THE BASICS

Before You Go

Visitors entering Spain should be in possession of a valid passport or, for EU citizens, an identity card. No visa is required for members of EU countries or US, Canadian or New Zealand citizens, but visitors from Australia do require a visa, which can be obtained on arrival for a period of up to 30 days. No vaccinations are necessary.

Getting There

By Air: Spain's national airline is Iberia. There are numerous scheduled flights to Barcelona and to Catalunya's other major airport, Girona. Visitors coming from the US will probably fly direct to Barcelona or Madrid, though sometimes it is cheaper to fly to London or another European city first, then get a connecting flight to Spain.

Scheduled flights leave all year round for Barcelona from Dublin and Belfast.

Visitors from Australia and New Zealand cannot get a direct flight to Spain, and will have to make a stopover at another European city.

A Madrid-Barcelona air shuttle service operates hourly from 6.45am-10.45pm.

By Car: There are various options for those wanting to take their own car to Southern Spain. Two ferry companies offer direct sailings to Bilbao and Santander from Britain: Brittany Ferries and P&O European Ferries. This eliminates the long – and expensive – drive through France.

Several ferry companies carry cars and passengers across the English Channel, with the quickest journeys being between Dover/Calais, and Folkestone/Boulogne. The hovercraft is even faster, crossing from Dover to Calais in just 35 minutes. Brittany Ferries offer crossings from Portsmouth, Plymouth and Poole directly to Brittany (St Malo and Roscoff).

The A 7 highway connects the Autopista del Mediterráneo with France, and the A 2 highway connects Barcelona to Zaragoza, Madrid and Bilbao. All the *autopistas* to Barcelona are toll roads.

By Coach: The main terminal is Estació del Nord ☎ **(93) 265 65 08**. Euroline's international coach services runs regular bus services to Barcelona from Britain and other European countries. Information and bookings in the UK can be made from 52 Grosvenor Gardens, London SW1W 0AU

☎ (0171) 730 8235.

By Train: Le Shuttle takes cars under the English Channel from Folkestone in 35 minutes. A connection can then be made at Paris with the Expresso Puerta del Sol, which leaves each night for Spain. Pedestrians can take the Eurostar from London through the Channel Tunnel, and must then change train stations in Paris (Gare du Nord to Austerlitz) to travel on either the Cerbère/Port Bou or the less frequent La Tour de Carol/Puigcerdà route.

There are various rail passes which offer substantial discounts. Details are obtainable from Rail Europe in New York (☎ 800 438 7245), or Eurotrain in London ☎ (0171) 730 3402, or British Rail European Information ☎ (0171) 834 2345.

Arriving

Barcelona's airport is located at El Prat de Llobregat, 12km (7.5 miles) south-west of the city; ☎ (93) 478 50 00.

There is an airport railway station, but a walk is involved. Trains leave regularly for Estació de Sants, starting at 5.43am and finishing at 10.13pm. The journey takes about 25 minutes.

A frequent bus service, the 'Aerobus', also operates (from Plaça de Catalunya: Monday to Friday 5.30am-10.15pm, weekends 6am-10.20pm. From the airport: Monday to Friday 6am-11pm, weekends 6.30am-10.50pm).

Taxis are the easiest option, but will cost up to 2 500ptas. Make for the official ranks outside each terminal.

A traditional tour of the town.

A-Z

Accidents and Breakdowns

If you are involved in an accident while driving in Spain you should exchange full details of insurance, addresses, etc. In an emergency, if you can find a telephone, ☎ 091.

When travelling in a hire car, contact the rental firm in the event of an accident or breakdown.

See also **Driving** and **Car Hire**

Accommodation *see p.92*

Airports *see* **Getting There p.110**

Banks

Banks are open 8.30/9am-2pm, Monday to Friday. Main branches are also open on Saturday from 9am-12.30/1pm. Between June and September most banks are closed on Saturdays.

Most major credit cards are accepted by hotels and department stores. Girobank operates an international cash card system which allows cash withdrawals on personal UK bank accounts.

Eurocheques backed up by a Eurocheque card can be used in banks, and to pay for goods in hotels, restaurants and shops. Most cheque cards, and Visa and Mastercard, can be used to withdraw cash from automatic cash machines.

Banks will usually change travellers' cheques, but charge high commission rates, and there are also specialist exchange bureaux. Exchange facilities, at competitive rates, are available at El Corte Inglés, a department store with its main Barcelona branch on Plaça Catalunya.

Bicycles

There are a number of cycle lanes in Barcelona which make this a viable mode of transport, though visitors should take care when cycling in the city. Town bikes, mountain bikes and tandems are available. Few bike-hire shops take credit cards.

Breakdowns *see* **Accidents**

Buses *see* **Transport**

Camping

There are about a dozen campsites within easy reach of Barcelona. For a free list of these sites, contact the Spanish National Tourist Office in your own country, or obtain one locally from any tourist office (*see* **Tourist Information Offices**).

Unauthorised camping is not recommended.

Car Hire

International and local car-hire companies are based in the city centre as well as at the airport. Make sure that collision damage waiver is included in the insurance. Automatics should be reserved in advance and are more expensive.

The lower age limit is usually 21, but in practice few international companies hire to drivers under 23, or even 25. Drivers must have held their full licence for at least a year.

With the exception of Avis, there is an upper age limit of 60-65. Unless paying by credit card, a substantial cash deposit is usually required. If you are driving a car that has obviously been hired, take extra precautions when parking it to deter thieves, and never leave anything of value inside.

See also **Accidents and Breakdowns** and **Driving**

Children

Apart from the beaches, attractions in Barcelona likely to appeal to children include:
Museu de la Ciència, C/Teodor Roviralta 55 (*see* p.72). Science museum with lots of interactive displays and a planetarium.
Parc d'atraccions de Montjuïc, Avda Miramar (*see* p.55). Straightforward funfair and park with great views.
Port Aventura, near Salou. Outside the city; a huge highly-rated theme park based on five different cultures, with all the thrills and spills associated with complexes of this kind.
Tibidabo Funfair, Parc d'Atraccions del Tibidabo. Plaça Tibidabo 3-4 (*see* p.73). Fun park with amusements old and new, spread across landscaped gardens on Mount Tibidabo.
Parc Zoològic, Parc de la Ciutadella (*see* p.52). Includes a children's zoo and dolphin shows.
Aquàrium, Port Vell (*see* p.47). New state-of-the-art attraction, with vast marine tanks and the exciting shark tunnel.
IMAX cinema, Port Vell (*see* p.48). Experience films almost as if you were there on a massive 180° screen.

Climate *see* p. 88

Clothing

The people of Barcelona are fairly liberal in their attitudes to dress, although they are also keen on looking smart. In the evenings, in particular, they make a great effort. Places of worship and museums will often exclude those who are not dressed soberly. Hats are a good idea at the height of summer, particularly in the early afternoon.

Women's Sizes

UK	8	10	12	14	16	18
Europe	34	36	38	40	42	44
US	6	8	10	12	14	16

Men's Suits

UK/US	36	38	40	42	44	46
Europe	46	48	50	52	54	56

Men's Shirts

UK/US	14	14.5	15	15.5	16	16.5	17
Europe	36	37	38	39/40	41	42	43

Men's Shoes

UK	7	7.5	8.5	9.5	10.5	11
Europe	41	42	43	44	45	46
US	8	8.5	9.5	10.5	11.5	12

Women's Shoes

UK	4.5	5	5.5	6	6.5	7
Europe	38	38	39	39	40	41
US	6	6.5	7	7.5	8	8.5

Consulates

Australia
Gran Vía Carles III 98
☎ (93) 330 94 96

Canada (Embassy: there is no Consulate in Barcelona)
Calle Núñez de Balboa 35, 28001 Madrid
☎ (91) 431 43 00

Ireland
Gran Vía Charles III 94
☎ (93) 491 50 21

UK
Avda Diagonal 477
☎ (93) 419 90 44

USA
Passeig de la Reina Elisend 23
☎ (93) 280 22 27

Crime

There is no need to be unduly concerned about serious crime in Barcelona, but pick-pocketing and bag-snatching are rife and it is advisable to take sensible precautions and be on your guard at all times. Ploys such as 'helpfully' pointing out a stain on your jacket to distract you are com-monplace.

- Carry as little money and as few credit cards as possible, and leave any valuables in the hotel safe.

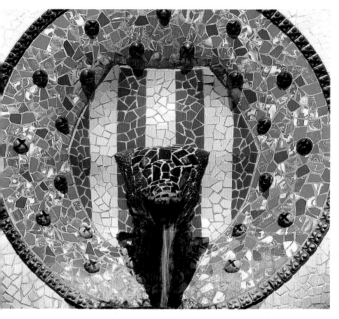

Detail of a fountain, Parc Güell.

- Carry wallets and purses in secure pockets, wear body belts, or carry handbags across your body or firmly under your arm.
- Cars are a target for opportunists, so never leave your car unlocked.
- Beware of diversionary tactics by 'professional' petty thieves.
- If you do have anything stolen, report it immediately to the local police and collect a copy of the report so that you can make an insurance claim.
- If your passport is stolen, report it to your Consulate or Embassy at once (*see* **Consulates**).

Currency *see* **Money**

Customs and Entry Regulations
There is no limit on the importation into Spain of tax-paid

goods bought in an EU country, provided they are for personal consumption, with the exception of alcohol and tobacco which have fixed limits governing them.

Disabled Visitors

Spain is not the most accessible country for disabled travellers, and public transport is particularly difficult for wheelchair users. The *Michelin Red Guide España-Portugal* indicates which hotels have facilities for the disabled.

In Britain, RADAR, at 12 City Forum, 250 City Road, London EC1V 8AF ☎ **(0171) 250 3222**, publishes fact sheets as well as an annual guide to facilities and accommodation overseas.

The Spanish National Tourist Office in your own country is a good source of information, and you are also advised to check with hotels and tour operators that your individual needs can be met.

Driving

It is not recommended for visitors to drive in Barcelona, as the roads are busy and parking difficult. Drivers should carry a full national or preferably international driving licence, insurance documents including a green card (no longer compulsory for EU members but strongly recommended), registration papers for the car, and a nationality sticker for the car rear.

A bail bond or extra insurance cover for legal costs is also worth investing in. Without a bail bond the car could be impounded and the driver placed under arrest.

The minimum age for driving is 18, and cars drive on the right. Away from main roads, cars give way to those approaching from the right. Drivers and passengers must wear seatbelts at all times.

Speed traps are used, and if you are caught, the police are likely to impose a hefty fine. Speed limits are as follows:

- Maximum on urban roads: 50kph/31mph
- Maximum on other roads: 90kph or 100kph/56 or 62mph
- Dual carriageways: 120kph/75mph.

Also note that Spanish motorways have tolls.

Electric Current

The voltage in Spain is usually 220 or 225V. Plugs and sockets are of the two-pin variety, and

Steps leading up to the Hall of Columns, Parc Güell.

adaptors are generally required. North American appliances will probably also need a transformer.

Embassies *see* Consulates

Emergencies
National Police ☎ 091
Police Tourist Assistance
☎ (93) 301 90 60
City Police ☎ 092
Fire service: ☎ 080
Emergency medical assistance and ambulance ☎ 061

Etiquette
As in most places in the world, when visiting churches and museums visitors are expected to dress appropriately, covering upper legs and arms. Greeting people with *bon dia* (good day) is customary.

Guidebooks *see* Maps

Health
UK nationals should carry a Form E111, which is produced by the Department of Health, and entitles the holder to free urgent treatment for accident or illness in EU countries (forms are available from post offices in Britain). The treatment will have to be paid for in the first instance, but the money can be reclaimed later.

Detail of Columbus Monument.

All foreign nationals, including those from the UK, are advised to take out comprehensive insurance cover, and to keep any bills, receipts and invoices to support any claim.

Lists of doctors can be obtained from hotels, chemists (*farmàcies*) and consulates, and first aid and medical advice is also available at chemists from pharmacists, who are highly trained and can dispense drugs which are available only on prescription in other countries.

You can get the address of an

English-speaking doctor from your hotel, consulate, the police station, *farmàcies* or the nearest tourist office.

Hours see Opening Hours

Information see Tourist Information Offices

Language
Around 60 per cent of the population of Barcelona speak Catalan rather than Castillian Spanish, and all streets are signposted and named in Catalan. Having said that, any knowledge of Spanish will stand you in good stead, and if you can manage a few words of Catalan, so much the better.

Lost Property
Municipal Lost Property Office: Servi de Troballes, Ajuntament, C Ciutat 9, open

Monday to Friday 9am-2pm
☎ (93) 317 38 79.
  Lost property on the Metro:
☎ (93)318 70 74.
  Lost property on buses:
☎ (93) 336 61 61.

Maps
There is a range of Michelin road atlases and sheet maps of Barcelona and the surrounding area. The Michelin **Map 443** North East Spain covers Catalunya, and is useful when planning excursions from Barcelona. It also includes a street plan of the city, with a street index. The spiral-bound *Michelin Road Atlas: Spain and Portugal* covers the whole of the Iberian peninsula, Michelin **Map 990** covers the whole of Spain and is useful for route-planning if driving to Barcelona.

English	Spanish	Catalan
Yes	Sí	Si
No	No	No
Please	Por favor	Si us plau
Thank you	Gracias	Gràcies
Hello	Hola	Hola
Good morning	Buenos dias	Bon dia
Goodbye	Adiós	Adéu
How much	¿ Cuánto?	¿ Quant?
Where?	¿ Dónde?	¿ On?
I don't understand	No Entiendo	No ho entenc
Do you speak English?	¿Habla (usted) ingles?	¿Parleu anglès?

The *Michelin Green Guide Spain* contains useful information on the sights and attractions in Barcelona and also describes many of the towns and villages surrounding the city which you may be interested in visiting. The *Michelin Green Guide Barcelone et la Catalogne* (French edition) and *Green Guide Cataluña* (Spanish edition) cover the sights and attractions in Barcelona and Catalunya, and include numerous maps. The *Michelin Red Guide España/Portugal* lists accommodation and restaurants.

Medical Care *see* Health

Money
The Spanish unit of currency is the peseta, with notes in denominations of 1 000, 2 000, 5 000 and 10 000 pesetas, and coins of 1, 5, 10, 25, 50, 100, 200 and 500 pesetas.

There is no restriction on bringing currency below the level of one million pesetas into or out of the country, but perhaps the safest way to carry large amounts of money is in travellers' cheques, which are widely accepted. Exchange counters are found at airports, terminals and larger railway stations, at the El Corte Inglés department store and at banks (see **Banks**).

Lost or stolen travellers' cheques and credit cards should be reported immediately to the issuing company, with a list of numbers, and the police should also be informed.

Newspapers
There are several Spanish daily papers sold in Barcelona, including *El País*, *El Mundo*, *ABC* and *Diario*. *El Mundo* and *El País* have useful entertainment listings supplements. *La Vanguardia* and *Avui* are both Catalan papers.

If you are looking for English-language media, *Lookout* and *In Spain* are both monthly magazines, produced primarily for the English-speaking community.

British and other foreign newspapers are widely available.

Opening Hours
Shops normally open at 9.30/10am, close for lunch at 1.30/2pm, and then reopen at 4.30/5pm. They stay open till 8/8.30pm, or sometimes later in the summer.
Chemists (*farmàcia*) are usually open from 9.30am-2pm and from 4.30pm-8pm, Monday to Saturday. Those branches which open at night, on

Sundays and on public holidays are listed in the window of each chemist.

Museums and galleries tend to open between 10am-1.30pm and 4-7pm, with several variations, while many **churches** open only for the early morning or evening service each day.

See also **Banks** and **Post Offices**

Photography

Good-quality film and camera equipment are available in Barcelona, and facilities for fast processing are plentiful, although this is often expensive.

Before taking photographs in museums and art galleries it is wise to check with staff as photography is often restricted in these places.

Police

There are three types of police: the Guardia Civil, the Policía Municipal and the Policía Nacional. The Policía Municipal are usually sympathetic to tourists with problems.
See **Emergencies**

Post Offices

Barcelona's main post office (*Correos*), Plaça Antòni López, is at the end of Vía Laietana ☎ 318 38 31. It is open to the public from Monday to Saturday, 8.30am-9pm. Branch offices are open from 9am-2pm.

Poste restante mail should be sent to the person (surname underlined) at Lista de Correos, followed by the name of the town and province. Take a passport along as proof of identity when collecting mail.

Stamps (*sellos*) can be bought at post offices and at tobacconists (*estancos*). Normal post boxes are yellow, but urgent mail can be posted in red post boxes, stamped accordingly; ask at a tobacconist (*estanco*).

Public Holidays

New Year's Day: 1 January
Epiphany: 6 January
Good Friday to Easter Monday
Labour Day: 1 May
Sant Joan (Midsummer Day): 24 June
Corpus Christi: 2nd Thursday after Whitsun
Assumption Day: 15 August
Diada Nacional de Catalunya (Catalan National Day): 11 September
Día de la Hispanidad (National Day): 12 October
All Saints' Day: 1 November
Constitution Day: 6 December
Immaculate Conception: 8 December
Fira de Santa Llúcia: 13

December
Christmas Day: 25 December
Boxing Day: 26 December
There are also other feasts and
public holidays which are cele-
brated locally, when almost
everything shuts down, such as
St Joseph's Day: 19 March
St James' Day: 25 July

Public Transport
see **Transport**

Religion
Spain is a Catholic country,
and there are daily services in
the churches and cathedrals.
The location of churches and
the times of services are best
checked locally.
See **Tourist Information
Offices**

Smoking
Legislation protects the rights
of non-smokers over those of
smokers in Spain these days,
and smoking is banned in
many public places.

Stamps see Post Offices

Taxis see Transport

Telephones
Spanish public telephones
have instructions in English
and take 5, 25 or 100 peseta
coins (newer booths also take
50 and 500 peseta coins), or

phonecards of 1 000 or 2 000
pesetas – which can be bought
at tobacconists (*estancos*), or
post offices – and credit cards.
International calls may be
made either in telephone
booths, or at a *Telefónica* office
where you pay after the call.
As in most countries,
telephone calls made from
hotels may be more straightforward and convenient, but they
are more expensive.
The international dialling
code for Barcelona: ☎ 0034 3
To call Barcelona from within
Spain: ☎ 93
Directory Enquiries: ☎ 003
Area codes: ☎ 009
International operator: ☎ 008
for Europe; ☎ 005 for the rest
of the world.
When making international
calls from Barcelona, ☎ 07,
wait for the dialling tone, and
then dial the appropriate
country code:
Australia: ☎ 00 61
Canada: ☎ 00 1
Ireland: ☎ 00 353
New Zealand: ☎ 00 64
UK: ☎ 00 44
USA: ☎ 00 1
To call Spain from abroad,
☎ 00 34.

Time Difference
Spanish standard time is GMT
plus one hour. Spanish
summer time begins on the last

Ornate balconies and façade.

Sunday in March at 2am when the clocks go forward an hour (the same day as British Summer Time), and it ends on the last Sunday in October at 3am when the clocks go back again.

Tipping

In Spain it is usual to tip between 5-10 per cent of the bill at bars, cafés and restaurants, even though bills already include a service charge. The tip is related to customer satisfaction. Porters, doormen, taxi drivers and cinema usherettes all expect a financial token of appreciation.

Tourist Information Offices

The Spanish National Tourist Office (SNTO) is an excellent first source of information for your holiday. The offices are well stocked with leaflets providing information on excursions, transport, entertainment, facilities for the disabled, and exhibitions, as well as accommodation and restaurants. Many free leaflets and brochures are available and guide books and maps are for sale.

Spanish Tourist Offices abroad:

Australia
203 Castlereagh Street, Suite 21a, PO Box A685, Sydney, NSW
☎ **(02) 264 7966**

Canada
2 Bloor Street West, 34th Floor, Toronto, Ontario M4W 3E2
☎ **(416) 961 3131**

UK
22-23 Manchester Square, London W1M 5AP
☎ **(0171) 486 8077**

USA
666 Fifth Avenue 35th, New York, NY10103
☎ **(212) 265 8822**
Water Tower Place, Suite 915 East, 845 North Michigan Avenue, Chicago, IL 60611
☎ **(312) 642 1992**

In Barcelona, the main office of the City Tourist Board is at Plaça Catalunya 17
☎ **(93) 304 31 34** and that of the Catalan Regional Government at Gran Vía de les Corts Catalanes 658 ☎ **(93) 301 74 43**. Branch offices can be found elsewhere in the city, including the airport
☎ **(93) 478 50 00**.

Tourist Information is also available on ☎ **901 300 600**.

During the summer, helpful and multi-lingual information officers, known as 'Red Jackets' because of their distinctive uniforms, roam around the Gothic Quarter and other main tourist areas, from 9am-9pm.

Tours

Two companies, Julià Tours and Pullman Tours, provide coach tours of the city, details of which can be obtained from tourist information offices.

The *Bus Turístic* (*see* **Transport**) is a good way of seeing the main sights. Occasionally, historic walking tours are organised by the Museu d'Història de la Ciutat (*see* p.27).

Transport

Barcelona's integrated public transport system is largely based on the metro and bus services. Free transport maps are available from any tourist office. Several types of travel-cards (*targetas*), valid on both the metro and buses, are available and are much more economical than purchasing single tickets. *Targetas* must be punched in the automatic machines before boarding a train or bus.

Metro This is run by the city transport authority (TMB). The central TMB information office is at Metro Universitat ☎ **(93) 318 70 74**; open 8am-7pm Monday to Friday. There are five colour-coded subway lines. Trains run from 5am-11pm Monday to Thursday; 5am-1am on Fridays, Saturdays and the day before a holiday (*see* **Public Holidays**); and 6am-midnight on Sunday.

Buses Most buses run from 5.30am-11pm, although there is a special night service. For information about buses, ☎ **(93) 318 70 74**.

Between Easter and the end of October a tourist bus, *Bus Turístic* (No 100) runs on a circular route, starting on Plaça Catalunya, taking in the main sights and attractions. *Targetes* are not valid on this and tickets must be purchased on board.

Trains The Catalan government railway (FGC) operates one of the underground railway lines, and also serves the surrounding countryside. For further details contact: FGC Information, Vestibule, Plaça Catalunya Station ☎ **(93) 205 15 15**.

In addition to the FGC system, the Spanish Railways (RENFE) run services throughout the country. Children under three can travel free on trains, and those under seven are charged only half price. For details of services and discounts on train fares, enquire at Spanish Railways RENFE ☎ **(93) 490 02 02** (domestic trains); ☎ **(93) 490 11 22** (international trains), or a tourist office in your own country or in Barcelona.

Taxis are a fairly economical alternative form of transport in Barcelona. They are painted black and yellow and can be hailed in the street when showing a green light on the roof. Taxi ranks can be found at railway and bus stations, the main squares, and various other locations throughout the city. Official rates are posted inside the cab. On top of the basic charge, there is a surcharge for night-time, weekends and public holidays. Very few drivers accept credit cards.

See also **Tourist Information Offices** and **Driving**

TV and Radio

TVE 1 and TVE 2 are Spain's two nationwide television channels. Barcelona also has Antena 3, Tele 5 and TV3.

The choice is a mixture of

Part of Barcelona's excellent metro system.

good live sports coverage, game shows, dubbed foreign-language films and series, and soap operas from the US, Australia, the UK and South America.

English radio programmes may be picked up on the BBC World Service on short-wave radio, as well as on the Torrejón American Airforce Base station at 100.2 FM.

Vaccinations see **Before You Go p.110**

Youth Hostels see **Accom-modation p.92**

INDEX